Excel 5.0 for Windows

James E. Shuman

Bellevue Community College

Wadsworth Publishing Company

I(T)P™ An International Thomson Publishing Company

Belmont • Albany • Bonn • Boston • Cincinnati • Detroit • London • Madrid • Melbourne
Mexico City • New York • Paris • San Francisco • Singapore • Tokyo • Toronto • Washington

Computer Information Systems Publisher: Kathy Shields
Assistant Editor: Tamara Huggins
Supplements Editor: Sherry Schmitt
Editorial Assistant: Joan Paterson
Production Services Coordinator: Gary Mcdonald
Production: Gary Palmatier, Ideas to Images
Print Buyer: Diana Spence
Text Designer: Gary Palmatier
Copy Editor: Anna Huff
Technical Illustrator: Ideas to Images
Signing Representative: Karen Buttles
Cover: Ark Stein, The Visual Group
Compositor: Ideas to Images
Printer: Courier Companies, Inc.

 This book is printed on acid-free recycled paper.

For more information, contact Wadsworth Publishing Company.

Wadsworth Publishing Company
10 Davis Drive
Belmont, California 94002
USA

International Thomson Publishing Europe
Berkshire House 168-173
High Holborn
London, WC1V7AA
England

Thomas Nelson Australia
102 Dodds Street
South Melbourne 3205
Victoria, Australia

Nelson Canada
1120 Birchmount Road
Scarborough, Ontario
Canada M1K 5G4

International Thomson Editores
Campos Eliseos 385, Piso 7
Col. Polanco
11560 México D.F. México

International Thomson Publishing GmbH
Königswinterer Strasse 418
53227 Bonn
Germany

International Thomson Publishing Asia
221 Henderson Road
#05-10 Henderson Building
Singapore 0315

International Thomson Publishing Japan
Hirakawacho Kyowa Building, 3F
2-2-1 Hirakawacho
Chiyoda-ku, Tokyo 102
Japan

ISBN: 0-534-30554-7

Contents

Preface

The Windows Workshop is a series of Windows applications books. Currently, the series includes Windows, Word, WordPerfect, Excel, Quattro Pro, Lotus, Access, and Paradox. These books focus on the fundamental features of each application and provide a way for students to become fairly proficient within a short time. The emphasis is on how the application can be used to develop documents, analyze information, and solve problems. A case study, Adventure Tours, is used to provide realism and continuity throughout the series. These applications are available as individual books or as a custom-published combination of books. For example, if your course includes Word, Excel, and Access, these could be combined into a single title. In fact, you can choose individual chapters, so you might want to include Chapter 1 from the Windows book, which provides an introduction to Windows.

TO THE INSTRUCTOR

The purpose of this text is to help students develop the skills necessary to create documents and charts using Microsoft Excel 5.0 for Windows. As students create documents they learn the basics of working with spreadsheets as well as the most commonly used features of Microsoft Excel 5.0. The documents students will develop and analyze include budgets, sales forecasts, survey reports, sales reports, and personal budgets.

This text provides a practical, hands-on approach to developing skills in the use of Excel 5.0 for Windows. The text requires active participation as students develop real-world applications. The emphasis is on learning by doing, a process that becomes exciting and motivating for students as they explore Microsoft Excel 5.0.

This text is presented as a self-paced tutorial designed to be used in a lab setting. A concept such as using functions, performing "what-if" analysis, or linking worksheets is introduced. The concept is explained and then followed by the actual steps, so students learn the "why" along with the "how." In each chapter students work through examples so that new commands are practiced as they are presented. Exercises are used to reinforce learning by requiring students to apply skills as they are learned. Figures duplicating the monitor display guide students through the operations involved in completing a particular exercise. This approach allows you, the instructor, to determine your level of involvement—from providing presentations that supplement the text material to acting as a resource person.

Chapters are organized as follows:

- Chapter objectives
- Self-paced tutorials to teach new commands and techniques
- Exercises to reinforce learning
- End-of-chapter materials: Key Terms, Review Questions, and Projects

Features and Benefits of This Text

Explanation of Underlying Concepts   Students gain an understanding of spreadsheets the creation of documents and charts, and Excel's graphical environment.

Sequential Instruction   Step-by-step instructions allow students to progress at their own pace. They learn the basic commands first and then move to more advanced features. This approach allows students to redo a section for reinforcement or review. Chapters may be completed in an open lab setting where the instructor need not be present and where students can aid one another in the learning process.

Extensive Use of Figures   Students can check what is displayed on the monitor with more than 100 figures provided in the text. These figures guide students through the sequential instruction.

Exercises   Once a command is learned, students are challenged to use the skill to complete a practical exercise.

Numerous Projects   End-of-chapter projects provide practical applications to stimulate interest, reinforce learning, and test acquired skills.

Student-Tested Approach   Students unfamiliar with computers are able to complete this text with minimal guidance. Students like the self-paced tutorial approach and the challenges provided by the exercises and projects.

Data Disk   The data disk (bundled with the Instructor's Manual) accompanying this text has several files that can be used by the students to complete the tutorials, exercises, and projects. Use of the data disk simulates a business environment. In addition, students are able to work with larger and more complex documents without having to spend time entering text.

Appendix   Provides a glossary and quick-reference section, including shortcut keys.

TO THE STUDENT

The purpose of this text is to help you develop the skills necessary to create documents and charts using Microsoft Excel 5.0 for Windows. You will be developing the most commonly used documents: budgets, sales forecasts, survey reports, sales analyses, and personal budgets. You will learn how to enter numbers quickly and perform calculations. You will also learn how to enhance the appearance of documents by using bold and italic type, borders and patterns, different type designs and type sizes, and by formatting numbers.

This text provides a practical, hands-on approach to developing skills in the use of Microsoft Excel 5.0 for Windows. The text allows you to work at your own pace through step-by-step tutorials. A concept is presented, such as creating a chart. The concept is explained then followed by the actual steps. Throughout the text, figures show appropriate screen displays to help keep you on track. Examples, exercises, and projects will reinforce your learning.

To learn the most from this text you should:

- Proceed slowly: Accuracy is more important than speed.

- Understand what is happening with each step before continuing to the next step.

- After finishing a process, ask yourself: Can I do the process on my own? If the answer is no, review the steps.

- Check your screen display with the figures in the text.

Enjoy learning Excel 5.0 for Windows!

ACKNOWLEDGMENT

The author would like to thank Heidi Sewall for her detailed review of the manuscript and thoughtful suggestions.

1

Introduction to Spreadsheets and Microsoft Excel 5.0

- Describe the parts of a spreadsheet

- Distinguish between a spreadsheet, workbook, worksheet, and document

- Use Excel to develop spreadsheet documents

- Distinguish between text, numbers, formulas, and functions

- Use the SUM function and the AutoSum tool

- Save, print, open, and close worksheet documents

- Format cells and change column widths

- Use the Excel Help feature

Microsoft Excel 5.0 is an extremely powerful spreadsheet program that is used with **Microsoft Windows**. A **spreadsheet program** is useful when you are developing documents that include numbers and calculations.

Figure 1.1 shows three documents developed using the Excel program: a monthly budget, an income forecast, and a survey form. These **documents** have three important features in common.

- They use numbers.
- They include calculations (such as totals).
- They are laid out in rows and columns.

1.1

Three documents

ADVENTURE TOURS
Projected Budget (Eastside Office)

	Jan	Feb	Mar	Apr	May	Jun	Total
INCOME							
Tours	30000	30000	30000	30000	30000	30000	180000
Members	200	200	200	200	200	200	1200
Total	30200	30200	30200	30200	30200	30200	181200
EXPENSES							
Salaries	20000	20000	20000	20000	20000	20000	120000
Rent	500	500	500	500	500	500	3000
Utilities	200	200	200	200	200	200	1200
Supplies	300	300	300	300	300	300	1800
Ads	800	800	800	800	800	800	4800
Travel	2000	2000	2000	2000	2000	2000	12000
Other	400	400	400	400	400	400	2400
Total	24200	24200	24200	24200	24200	24200	145200
PROFIT	6000	6000	6000	6000	6000	6000	36000

Monthly Budget

INCOME FORECAST BY OFFICE

	1995	1996	1997
Downtown	$450,000	500,000	540,000
Eastside	300,000	380,000	450,000
Total	750,000	880,000	990,000

Income Forecast

HOW LIKELY ARE YOU TO TAKE THE FOLLOWING TOURS WITHIN THE NEXT YEAR?

	Rafting	Trekking	Heli-ski	Safari	Mountain bike
Extremely	50	90	10	20	40
Very	75	65	15	25	60
Not very	25	35	20	35	80
Not at all	60	20	165	130	30
Total:	210	210	210	210	210

Survey Results

The Excel program is specifically designed to be used in developing these types of documents. Figure 1.2 shows the budget as it was developed in Excel. Notice that the Excel program is also laid out in rows and columns. Notice, too, that each number has a precise location in a particular row and column and that some of the numbers are the result of calculations. The Excel program makes it easy for you to enter numbers and perform calculations as you develop these types of documents. In addition, once you have developed a document, you can easily make changes in the numbers, and Excel will quickly update the calculations. This allows you to perform what-if analysis such as: What would happen to our profit if income increased by 10 percent or we decreased our advertising expenses by 5 percent? Another important feature of Excel is that you can create a chart using the numbers in the spreadsheet document. Figure 1.3 shows a chart using the income forecast numbers; you could also print out the numbers and the chart as one document.

1.2

The budget as developed in Excel

	A	B	C	D	E	F	G	H	I
1				ADVENTURE TOURS					
2				Projected Budget (Eastside Office)					
3									
4		Jan	Feb	Mar	Apr	May	Jun	Total	
5	INCOME								
6	Tours	30000	30000	30000	30000	30000	30000	180000	
7	Members	200	200	200	200	200	200	1200	
8	Total	30200	30200	30200	30200	30200	30200	181200	
9									
10	EXPENSES								
11	Salaries	20000	20000	20000	20000	20000	20000	120000	
12	Rent	500	500	500	500	500	500	3000	
13	Utilities	200	200	200	200	200	200	1200	
14	Supplies	300	300	300	300	300	300	1800	
15	Ads	800	800	800	800	800	800	4800	
16	Travel	2000	2000	2000	2000	2000	2000	12000	
17	Other	400	400	400	400	400	400	2400	
18	Total	24200	24200	24200	24200	24200	24200	145200	
19									
20	PROFIT	6000	6000	6000	6000	6000	6000	36000	

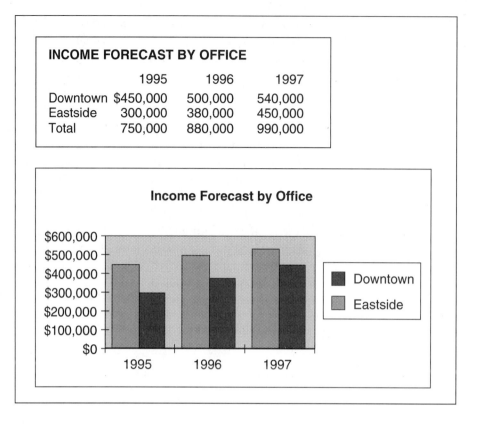

SPREADSHEETS, WORKBOOKS, AND WORKSHEETS

Several companies make spreadsheet programs. *Spreadsheet* is a generic word that refers to a computer-based program used to develop documents that are laid out in rows and columns and consist primarily of numbers and calculations. These documents are called **worksheets**. Excel organizes worksheets into workbooks. A **workbook** is like an electronic three-ring binder. Thus, it provides an easy way to group your work. You can have several workbooks, each with several worksheets. For example, a company could have one workbook that contains all of the sales worksheets and another workbook that contains all of the payroll worksheets. In this textbook the focus will be on developing worksheets. In Chapter 6 you will learn how to work with several worksheets in one workbook.

GETTING STARTED WITH EXCEL 5.0

Microsoft Excel 5.0 works with Microsoft Windows. Therefore, you need to start the Windows program in order to start Excel.

1. **Start Windows.**

Figure 1.4 shows the Program Manager screen in Windows and the Microsoft Office program group icon, where the Excel 5.0 program icon is located. (*Note*:

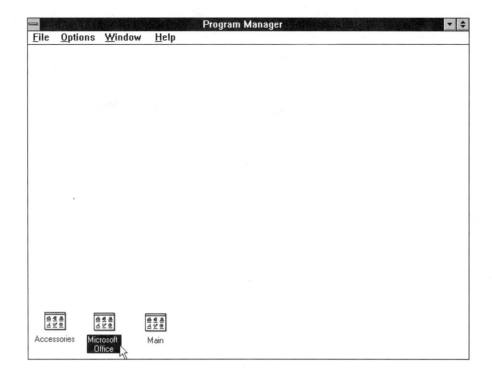

The procedure for starting Excel may vary according to the setup of your computer. These instructions assume the Excel group icon is in the Microsoft Office program group. Your setup may have this icon within another program group such as one called Windows Applications. If necessary, check with your instructor or lab assistant for further instructions on starting Excel.)

2. Double-click on the Microsoft Office program group icon (or the appropriate one for your computer setup).

The Microsoft Office program group window is opened, as shown in Figure 1.5. (Your screen may look different.) Several icons, including the Excel program icon, are within this window. You need to select the Excel program icon.

3. Double-click on the Microsoft Excel program icon (see Figure 1.5).

The Excel 5.0 spreadsheet program appears. Because this is a Windows application, many of the parts of the screen are the same as those shown on the Windows screen. Refer to Figure 1.6 as you read the following description of the parts of the Excel screen.

Workbook Window

- Title bar. The **title bar** displays the title of the program, Microsoft Excel. Also, the title bar displays the name of the workbook. If you have created and saved a document, the file name you used will be displayed. If you have not saved a document, the name **Book1** appears. If you open another document window, Book2 appears, and so forth.

- Control-menu box. The **control-menu box** is used to exit the program and to switch to another window or program.

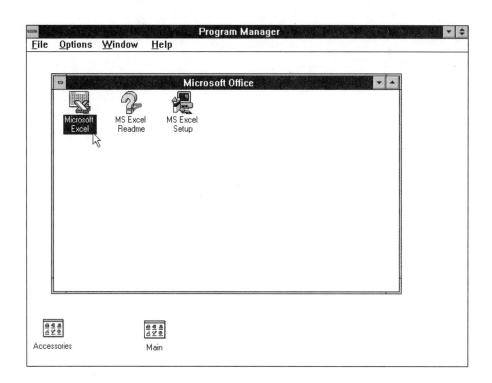

- Minimize button. The **minimize button** is used to reduce the window to an icon.

- Restore button. The **restore button** is used to restore the window to its previous size. (*Note:* The Excel workbook window is currently maximized. When you click on the restore button, it changes to a **maximize button** so that the window can be maximized again.)

- Menu bar. The **menu bar** lists the menus that contain the commands, such as Save and Print, that are used in Excel.

- Toolbars. The **Standard** and **Formatting toolbars** display the tools that are used as shortcuts in performing functions such as opening a new document or printing a document and changing the appearance of data by using bold or italic type, inserting dollar signs and commas, and other formatting features. (*Note:* Figure 1.6 shows the Standard and Formatting toolbars. Others, such as the Chart toolbar, may also appear on your screen.)

- Reference bar. The **reference bar** displays the name of the cell (A1) that is currently selected on the worksheet.

- Formula bar. The **formula bar** displays the entry, if any, for the selected location. Currently, no entry is in cell A1.

- Status bar. The left side of the **status bar** displays the current activity, such as printing; it also displays information about selected commands. The right side of the bar indicates what functions have been turned on, such as CAPS, which indicates that the [Caps Lock] key has been pressed and that text will be displayed in uppercase letters.

1.6

The Excel workbook window

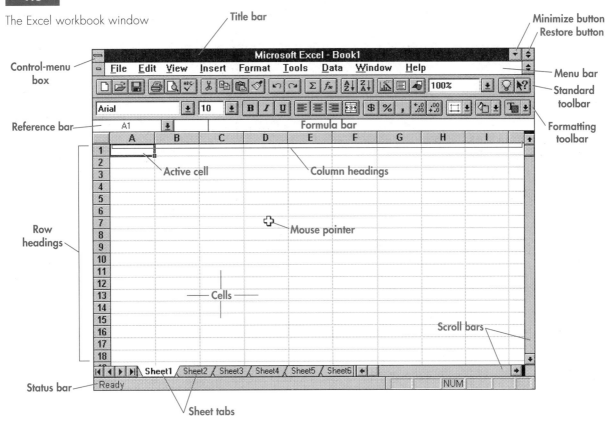

- Column headings (A, B, . . ., I). **Column headings** are used to identify the columns.

- Row headings (1, 2, . . ., 18). **Row headings** are used to identify the rows.

- Cells (A1, A2, A3, . . .). A **cell** is where a row and column intersect. Any data you type is entered into a cell.

- Active cell. The **active cell** is the cell that is currently selected (surrounded by a darkened border).

- Mouse pointer. The **mouse pointer** is used to select a cell or cells.

- Scroll bars. **Scroll bars** are used to scroll the window to view a different part of the worksheet.

- Sheet tabs. **Sheet tabs** are used to move from one worksheet in the workbook to another.

MOVING AROUND THE WORKSHEET

At any one time, you can see only a small part of the entire worksheet. The Excel worksheet is 256 columns wide and up to 16,384 rows deep. The columns are identified by letters: A, B, C, and so on. After column Z comes

AA, AB, AC, et cetera. The rows are identified by numbers: 1, 2, 3, and so forth. Where the rows and columns intersect are called cells. Each cell has a name determined by its column and row. Thus, where column A and row 1 intersect is cell A1; where column D and row 17 intersect is cell D17. To select a cell prior to entering data, you point to the cell with the mouse pointer, which is shaped like a cross, and click the mouse button. Or you can use the cell selector keys as listed here:

Press	To move
↑ ↓ ← →	Up or down one row or left or right one column
Home	To column A
←Enter	Down one row
Page Down	Down one screen
Page Up	Up one screen
Alt + Page Down	Right one screen
Alt + Page Up	Left one screen

(*Note:* When two keys are to be used together, such as Alt + Page Down, you hold down the first key and tap the second key. Then release the first key.)

Excel 5.0 allows you to change the function of certain keys. For example, depending on how Excel is set up on your computer, the ←Enter key could cause the cell selector to move down one row or stay on the same cell. If in the following steps these keys give you a different result from the one listed above, refer to "Transition Navigation Keys" in the appendix to learn how to change key settings.

Now take a few moments to practice using the cell selector keys to select various cells. Cell A1 should be selected. Notice that cell A1 has a darkened border around it and that A1 is displayed on the reference bar.

1. Press ↓ to move to cell A2.

Now the reference bar displays A2.

2. Press → to move to cell B2.

3. Press Page Down to move to cell B20 (down one screen).

4. Press Page Up to move back to cell B2 (up one screen).

5. Hold down Alt and press Page Down to move one screen to the right.

6. Press Home to move to column A.

7. On your own, use the cell selector keys to move around the worksheet.

8. When done, press Home to move to column A.

9. Select cell A1 (if it is not already selected).

ENTERING DATA INTO THE WORKSHEET

As we mentioned, data (text, numbers, formulas) are entered into cells. The process for entering data into a worksheet is to select the desired cell and type the data into the cell. Then press ⏎Enter or an arrow key. Figure 1.7 shows a simple worksheet you will duplicate.

1. **With cell A1 selected, type** Sales

Notice that as you type, the word *Sales* is displayed in the cell and on the formula bar.

2. **Press** →.

The cell selector moves to cell B1.

3. **Type** 500

4. **Press** ⏎Enter. **(Pressing** ⏎Enter **may move the cell selector down one row.)**

5. **Select cell A2.**

6. **Type** Expenses

This time instead of pressing ⏎Enter, press the → key. This will complete the entry and select the cell to the right.

7. **Press** → **to select cell B2.**

8. **Type** 400

1.7

A simple worksheet

9. Select cell A3.

10. Type Profit

11. Select cell B3.

ENTERING FORMULAS

At this point, you need to enter a formula to calculate the profit. Whenever possible, you should use formulas to perform calculations in a worksheet. This way, if a change is made in a number, the formula automatically updates the calculation. Excel allows you to use cell references and numbers in formulas. Formulas begin with an equal sign and must include at least one arithmetic operator. Examples of formulas are:

=B1+B2	Adds the numbers in cells B1 and B2 together
=A5+20	Adds 20 to the number in cell A5
=D12–D13	Subtracts the number in cell D13 from the number in cell D12
=A3*10–B4	Multiplies the number in cell A3 by 10 and subtracts the number in cell B4
=F20/3	Divides the number in cell F20 by 3
=C15*10%	Multiplies the number in cell C15 by 10%

The arithmetic operators are:

+   Addition

–   Subtraction

*   Multiplication

/   Division

^   Exponentiation (for example, 5^2 would be 5^2)

If you are using more than one operator in a formula, you need to understand which operation occurs first. The order of the operations is:

- Exponentiation

- Multiplication and division (left to right)

- Addition and subtraction (left to right)

An illustration, using numbers, of a formula with more than one operator is =10+4/2. If you evaluated the formula from left to right, the result would be 10 plus 4 is 14, and 14 divided by 2 is 7. However, Excel would perform the division first, resulting in 4 divided by 2 is 2, and 2 plus 10 is 12. You can use parentheses to change the order of operation. Operations within parentheses are calculated first. Thus, =(10+4)/2 would be evaluated as 10 plus 4 is 14, and 14 divided by 2 is 7.

When working with a spreadsheet, you want to use cell references instead of the numbers within the cells whenever possible. Thus, the formula to calculate the profit is =B1–B2. With cell B3 selected:

1. **Type** =B1–B2

Notice that as you enter a number, the formula bar changes to display four buttons. The × is called the cancel box and can be used to leave the editing mode without saving changes to the cell. The check mark is called the enter box and is used to accept the entry. The other two boxes are used for advanced functions in Excel 5.0. All cell entries must be completed, either by selecting a new cell, pressing ⏎Enter, or clicking on the cancel or the enter box. When an entry is completed, the boxes disappear from the formula bar.

2. **Point to the enter box on the formula bar.**

3. **Click the mouse button.**

The profit, 100, is displayed in the cell. However, notice that the formula bar displays the actual entry, =B1–B2. With this formula, any change in the numbers in B1 or B2 will be reflected in B3. Change the sales to 600.

4. **Select cell B1.**

5. **Type** 600

6. **Press** ⏎Enter.

The profit is recalculated to 200. Now, change the expenses to 450.

7. **On your own, change the expenses to 450, using the enter box on the formula bar to complete the entry.**

With the formula, you have created a relationship between cells B1 and B2, and cell B3. Thus, any changes you make in B1 or B2 are reflected in B3. Make another change to the expenses. Assume you anticipate that your expenses will be 80 percent of your sales. You can enter a formula in B2 to calculate the expenses no matter what the sales. With cell B2 selected:

8. **Type** =B1*80%

9. **Press** ⏎Enter.

With this formula, if you change the sales, the expenses and the profit will change accordingly.

EDITING DATA IN A WORKSHEET

Excel provides several ways for you to make changes in the data. To replace data in a cell, you select the cell and type the new entry. Change the word *Sales* to the word *Income*.

1. **Select cell A1.**

2. **Type** Income

3. **Press** ⏎Enter.

Move insertion point here

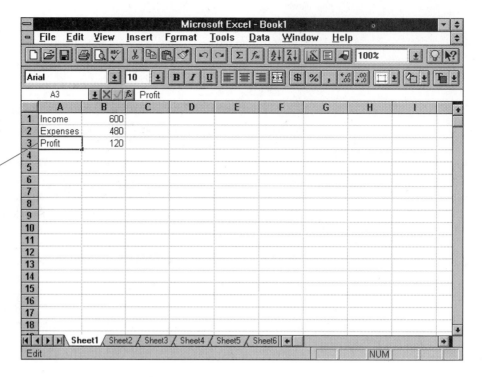

You can edit the contents of a cell without retyping the entire entry. For example, if you want to change *Profit* to *Our Profit*, you can insert the word *Our* into the cell.

4. **Point to the word *Profit* in cell A3.**

5. **Double-click the mouse button to display an insertion point.**

Notice how the pointer changes to an I-beam.

6. **Use the arrow keys to move the insertion point to just in front of the *P* in *Profit* (see Figure 1.8).**

7. **Type Our**

8. **Press the spacebar.**

9. **Click on the enter box to complete the entry.**

To delete an entry, you select the cell and press the Delete key. Delete the words *Our Profit*.

10. **Press Delete.**

The words *Our Profit* are deleted from the cell. You can undo several actions, including clearing the contents of a cell, by using the Undo command in the Edit menu.

11. **Click on Edit in the menu bar.**

12. **Click on Undo Clear.**

The words *Our Profit* reappear.

You can delete several entries at a time by highlighting the cells and pressing Delete. Continue by deleting all the entries. To highlight the cells, point to the

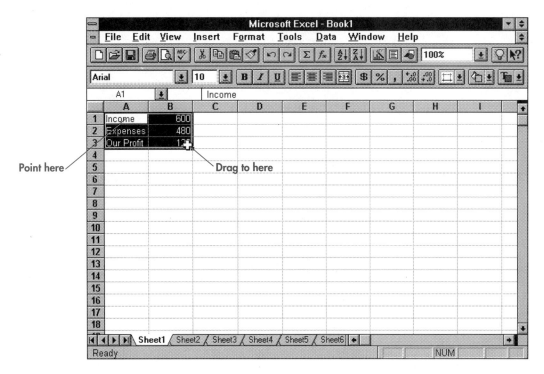

Point here

Drag to here

upper-left corner of the cell range (cell A1), hold down the mouse button, and drag the mouse pointer to the lower-right corner of the cell range (cell B3). Figure 1.9 shows this process.

13. Point to cell A1.

14. Hold down the mouse button.

15. Drag the mouse pointer to cell B3.

16. Release the mouse button.

17. Press [Delete].

18. Click on cell A1 to remove the highlight.

WORKING WITH LARGE TEXT AND NUMBER ENTRIES

In this section you will learn more about how to enter text and numbers in an Excel worksheet. You will also be developing a document for Adventure Tours, a company specializing in exotic vacations. The company uses Excel to develop several different types of documents, including budgets, income statements, and sales forecasts.

Excel makes a distinction between text entries and number entries. Following are important differences in working with text and numbers:

- Text entries can display across several cells.

- Number entries must fit within the cell.

- Text entries are left aligned in a cell (but can be changed to right or center aligned).

- Numbers are right aligned in a cell (but can be changed to left or center aligned).

Figure 1.10 shows a worksheet, a proposed budget, that includes several text and number entries. Notice that the heading, *Adventure Tours*, appears to be in cells A1 and B1. However, as the formula bar shows, the entire entry is in cell A1 only. The heading displays in cell B1, but this cell is actually empty. If you were to enter data in cell B1, the heading would be truncated. Figure 1.11 shows the heading after *1995* is entered into B1. Because there is an entry in B1, only the part of the heading that fits into A1 is displayed. Try this now. With cell A1 selected:

1. **Type** Adventure Tours

2. **Press** ⏎Enter.

Now make an entry into cell B1.

3. **Select cell B1.**

4. **Type** 1995

5. **Press** ⏎Enter.

With an entry in B1, the heading in A1 is truncated. The word *Tours* has not been erased; it simply cannot display in cell B1. To see that the entire heading is still intact, select cell A1.

6. **Select cell A1.**

Notice that the formula bar displays *Adventure Tours*. Now delete the entry in cell B1 so that the entire heading displays again.

1.10

A worksheet with several text and number entries

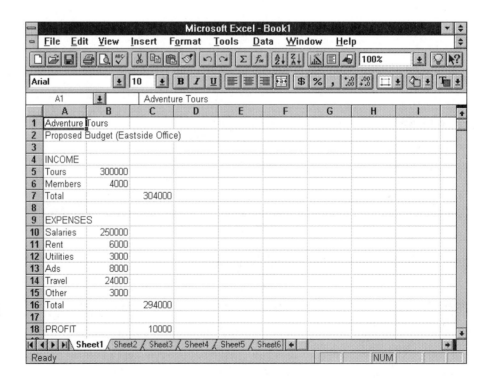

EXCEL 5.0 FOR WINDOWS

1.11

The heading, *Adventure Tours*, is truncated after 1995 is entered into cell B1

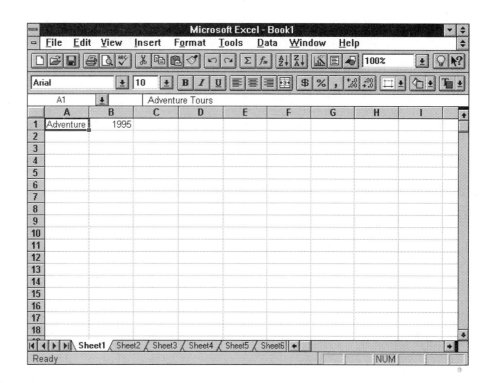

1.12

Three number entries

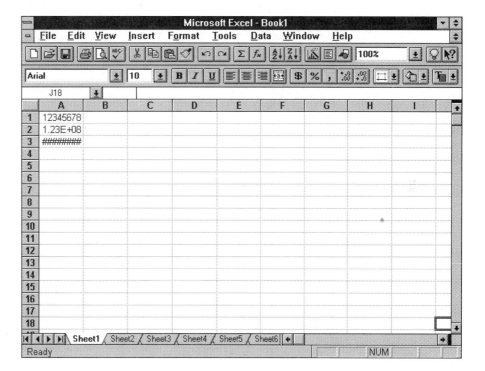

7. **Select cell B1.**

8. **Press** Delete .

Numbers that are larger than the cell width will not be displayed in adjacent cells. Rather, they will be displayed in scientific notation or as a series of hatch marks (#). Figure 1.12 shows three number entries. The entry in cell A1 fits within the cell. The entry in cell A2 is displayed in scientific notation because it is too large to fit within the cell. (*Note:* Scientific notation is used with very large numbers or very small numbers.) Cell A3 is filled with # signs, indicating that the number is too large to fit in the cell width. This also indicates that the number has been formatted to display additional symbols such as a dollar sign, comma, or decimal point. Formatted numbers do not display in scientific notation. Later in this chapter you will learn how to change the column width to accommodate large numbers.

The alignment of the entry in the cell is another distinction between text and numbers. As shown in Figure 1.10, the text entries are left aligned and the number entries are right aligned within the cells. This makes the worksheet easier to read by lining up the numbers and helping prevent text and numbers from running together.

Now take a few moments to complete part of the worksheet shown in Figure 1.10.

9. **Select cell A2.**

10. **Type** Proposed Budget (Eastside Office)

11. **Press** ⏎Enter.

12. **Select cell A4.**

13. **Type** INCOME

14. **Select cell A5.**

15. **On your own, complete the entries for cells A5, A6, B5, and B6.**

16. **Select cell A7.**

17. **Type** Total

18. **Select cell C7.**

19. **Type** =B5+B6

20. **Press** ⏎Enter.

21. **Enter EXPENSES into cell A9.**

22. **On your own, complete the entries for cells A10 through A15 and B10 through B15.**

23. **Enter Total into cell A16.**

24. **Select cell C16.**

At this point you could add the expenses using the formula =B10+B11+B12+B13+B14+B15. However, Excel provides an easier way to add a group of cells, the SUM function.

USING FUNCTIONS

Along with formulas, Excel provides an array of **functions** that can be used to perform calculations and statistical analysis. These functions are often shortcuts to long or complex formulas. For example, the formula =B10+B11+B12+B13+B14+B15 can be replaced with the function

=SUM(B10:B15). This **SUM function** adds the group of cells contained in the parentheses. The format for a function is:

=function name(cell range)

- ■ = indicates, along with the function name, that this is a function.

- ■ function name indicates the function.

- ■ (cell range) indicates the group of cells that the function will be performed on.

A cell range includes the first cell in the range, a colon, and the last cell in the range. The cell range is enclosed in parentheses, and there are no spaces in the function. Examples of other functions are:

=AVERAGE(C12:C17)	Calculates the average of the numbers in cells C12, C13, C14, C15, C16, and C17
=MAX(D2:H2)	Determines the highest number from the numbers in cells D2, E2, F2, G2, and H2
=MIN(D2:H2)	Determines the lowest number from the numbers in cells D2, E2, F2, G2, and H2

Now use the SUM function to total the expenses. With cell C16 selected:

1. **Type** =SUM(B10:B15)
2. **Press** ⏎Enter.

The result of the SUM function, 294000, is displayed in cell C16.

USING AUTOSUM

Excel provides a shortcut, the **AutoSum** tool, for summing a row or column of numbers.

You can click on the AutoSum button on the Standard toolbar, and Excel will automatically insert the SUM function. If you select a cell at the bottom of a column of numbers, Excel assumes that you want to add the column. If you select a cell to the right of a row of numbers, Excel assumes that you want to add the row. Try this now by summing the expenses and placing the total in cell B16.

1. **Select cell B16.**
2. **Click on the AutoSum button on the Standard toolbar (see Figure 1.13).**

A marquee (moving broken line) appears around the numbers in cells B10 through B15, and the formula bar displays =SUM(B10:B15).

3. **Click on the enter box.**

The total, 294000, appears in cell B16. In this case, you selected a cell at the bottom of a column of numbers, so Excel assumed you wanted to add the column and display the result in the selected cell. Before continuing, delete the entry in cell B16.

4. **Press** Delete.

Now complete the remainder of the worksheet.

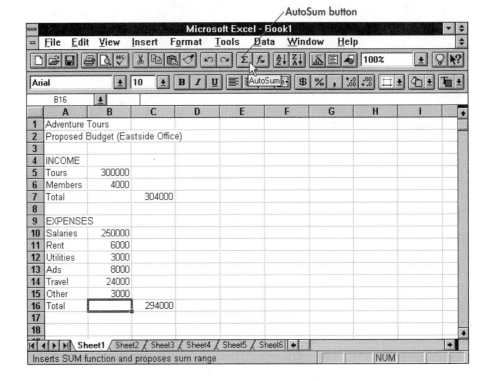

5. **Enter** PROFIT **into A18.**

6. **Select cell C18.**

To calculate the profit, you subtract the expenses from the income. The formula would be =C7–C16. Instead of typing this formula, you can select the cells to build the formula as follows:

7. **Type =**

8. **Press ↑ eleven times to select cell C7.**

9. **Type –**

10. **Press ↑ two times to select cell C16.**

11. **Click on the enter box.**

The formula is entered, and the result (10000) is displayed. This technique may seem more time-consuming than typing a formula. However, it is useful for long or complicated formulas because it can help prevent typing errors.

The worksheet is complete, and you can now save it. Before saving this worksheet, you will learn about commands.

WORKING WITH COMMANDS

Excel provides an array of **commands** that are used to carry out various processes such as saving and printing documents. These commands are listed in menus displayed in the menu bar. To choose a command, you click on the appropriate menu and then click on the command name. Complete the following steps to display the File menu commands and see how you can get information about each command:

1. **Point to File in the menu bar.**

2. **Click the mouse button.**

(*Note:* Another way to choose a menu is to hold down the [Alt] key and tap the underlined letter. For example, to choose the File menu, you can hold down [Alt] and tap the letter F.)

The File menu commands are displayed. Notice that the first command, New, is highlighted. On the status line at the bottom of the screen is a brief description of this command, Creates new document. Use [↓] to highlight the next command, Open.

3. **Press [↓] once.**

The description on the status line reads Opens saved document.

4. **On your own, highlight the other commands and read the status line for each one.**

Notice the file name(s) near the bottom of the list. (*Note:* Your screen may not show any.) These are the last documents that were used. They can be opened by clicking on the file name. This is useful as a shortcut for opening documents that are used often. The last command, Exit, quits the Excel program.

To choose a command, you either click on the command name or press the underlined letter; for instance, you would press P for the Print command. If you choose the wrong command, in most cases you can press the [Esc] key or click on the Cancel button to return to the worksheet. To remove a menu, you can click on the menu name.

5. **Point to File in the menu bar.**

6. **Click the mouse button to remove the menu.**

SAVING A WORKSHEET

To save a worksheet, you must save the workbook that contains the worksheet. Two commands are used to save a workbook, Save and Save As. The **Save As command** is usually used when you are saving a workbook for the first time or after you have already saved the workbook and want to save it again with a different file name. The **Save command** is used when you have previously saved a workbook and then made changes in it and you want to save it again with the same file name. When you save a workbook, you create a **file** that is saved to your data disk. You must indicate the name of the file and the disk drive where your data disk is located. A **file name** can be up to eight characters long and can include letters and numbers but not spaces. Your data disk will be in drive A or drive B, depending on your computer setup. Complete the following to save the worksheet with the file name at_budgt. (*Note:* The _ is an underscore character, not a space.)

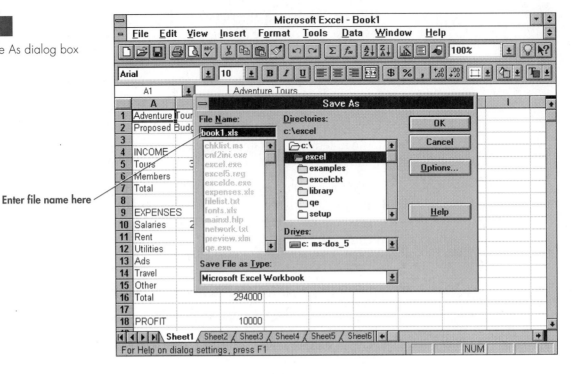

Enter file name here

1. **Insert the data disk in the appropriate drive.**

2. **Click on File in the menu bar.**

3. **Click on Save As.**

The Save As dialog box appears. Refer to Figure 1.14 as you read the following description of the parts of the dialog box:

■ File Name. This text box allows you to enter the name you want to use when saving the document. Currently, the file name is Book1.xls. Book1 is the name given to the workbook by Excel. The .xls is a file name extension automatically appended to any file name; it identifies the file as one that has been created using Excel. File name extensions are useful because later when you want to open a previously saved file, Excel displays a list of file names with the .xls extension. Notice that the file name is highlighted, indicating that if you type an entry it will replace the current file name.

■ Save File as Type. This list box allows you to choose from different file types. For instance, if you wanted to save the file so that it could be used with the Lotus program (another spreadsheet program) or with a Macintosh computer, you would display the list of options and choose the appropriate file type. Currently, the file type is Microsoft Excel Workbook, which means the file will be saved as an .xls Excel file. To see a list of the other file types, you would click on the down arrow.

■ Drives. This list box allows you to select the **drive** that contains the data disk you will save to. In Figure 1.14, the drive is set to c:. (*Note:*

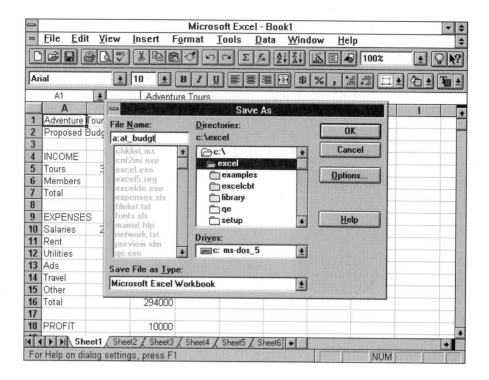

1.15

The entry to save the document to the disk in drive a with the file name at_budgt

Your setting may be different.) To display a list of the other drives, you would click on the down arrow.

- Directories. This lists the **subdirectory** (storage location on the drive) you are currently working with, if any. In Figure 1.14, the subdirectory is c:\excel. (*Note:* Your setting may be different.)

The most important things you need to specify in the Save As dialog box are the disk drive and the file name. In this book we assume you are working with drive A. If you are working with drive B, you need to specify B whenever the instruction is given to specify A. Now save the file to drive A (or B) with the file name at_budgt. Excel allows you to specify the drive along with the file name in the File Name text box. Thus, the entry is a:at_budgt (or b:at_budgt). You do not need to specify the file name extension. Excel will append it automatically. Figure 1.15 shows the completed entry. You can type the entry in uppercase or lowercase. With the file in the File Name box highlighted:

4. **Type** a:at_budgt (**or** b:at_budgt).

5. **Click on OK.**

The Summary Info dialog box appears, allowing you to enter information about the document, such as a title, subject, and key words. This information is useful when you are searching for a document and are not sure of the file name. It is also useful when you are sharing files with others in a workgroup environment. You do not need to make any entries in this dialog box.

6. **Click on OK.**

You are returned to the worksheet. Notice that the file name is now displayed on the title bar of the document window.

PRINTING A WORKSHEET

To print a document, you display the worksheet onscreen and choose the **Print command** from the File menu. Then complete the dialog box that appears onscreen. Excel allows you to preview the document before printing it. This is done with the Print Preview command in the File menu. First make sure the printer is ready; then preview how the document will print, and print it.

1. **Click on <u>F</u>ile in the menu bar.**

Notice the Print and Print Preview commands near the middle of the list.

2. **Click on Print Pre<u>v</u>iew.**

The print preview screen is displayed, showing how the document will print on a page. The document will print with gridlines, the workbook name at the top of the page, and the page number at the bottom of the page. In order to fit the entire page on the screen, the type size is very small. You can use the pointer to select an area of the page, and click the mouse button to enlarge it.

3. **Point above the workbook name at the top of the page (see Figure 1.16).**

Notice that the pointer changes to a magnifying glass.

4. **Click the mouse button.**

The selected area is enlarged to make it easier to read. You click the mouse button to return to the full page view.

5. **Click the mouse button.**

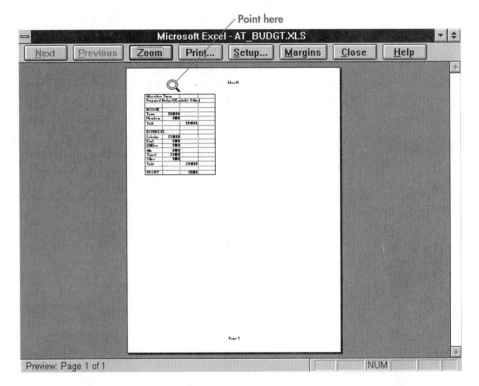

1.16

Enlarging an area of the page

The print preview screen has a button that allows you to print the document. Selecting this button is the same as choosing the Print command from the File menu.

6. Point to the Print button near the top of the screen.

7. Click the mouse button.

The Print dialog box appears. This box displays the name of the printer you are working with. It also allows you to, among other things, specify which pages of a multiple-page document you want to print and how many copies of the document you want to print.

8. Click on OK.

The document is printed, and you are returned to the worksheet.

CHANGING HOW A DOCUMENT PRINTS OUT

The printout you have just finished uses Excel's default settings. For example, Excel will print gridlines unless you specify otherwise. Figure 1.17 shows the document printed without gridlines. Figure 1.18 shows the document printed with gridlines and row and column headings. These changes can be made using the Page Setup dialog box. This dialog box can be displayed from the print preview screen. Complete the following steps to duplicate Figures 1.17 and 1.18:

1. Choose Print Preview from the File menu.

2. Click on the Setup button near the top of the screen.

1.17

The document printed without gridlines

ADVENTURE TOURS		
Projected Budget (Eastside Office)		
INCOME		
Tours	300000	
Members	4000	
Total		304000
EXPENSES		
Salaries	250000	
Rent	60000	
Utilities	3000	
Ads	8000	
Travel	24000	
Other	3000	
Total		294000
PROFIT		10000

1.18

The document printed with
row and column headings
and gridlines

	A	B	C	D
1	ADVENTURE TOURS			
2	Projected Budget (Eastside Office)			
3				
4	INCOME			
5	Tours	30000		
6	Members	4000		
7	Total		304000	
8				
9	EXPENSES			
10	Salaries	250000		
11	Rent	60000		
12	Utilities	3000		
13	Ads	8000		
14	Travel	24000		
15	Other	3000		
16	Total		294000	
17				
18	PROFIT		10000	

The Page Setup dialog box appears. At the top of the dialog box are four tabs that are used to display the various sections. The Gridlines and Row and Column Headings options are found in the section labeled Sheet.

3. **Click on the tab labeled Sheet.**

The Gridlines and Row and Column Headings options are located in the middle of this section. These options can be turned on and off by clicking on them. An X appears in the box next to them when they are turned on. Figure 1.19 shows that the Gridlines option is turned on.

4. **Point to Gridlines.**

5. **Click the mouse button to turn off this option. (The X should disappea**

6. **Click on OK to return to the print preview screen.**

7. **Click on the Zoom button to view the changes.**

The document now appears without the gridlines.

8. **On your own, print the document.**

Now turn on the Row and Column Headings option.

9. **On your own, display the print preview screen.**

10. **On your own, display the Page Setup dialog box.**

11. **Turn on the Row and Column Headings option.**

12. **Turn on the Gridlines option.**

13. **Return to the print preview screen.**

14. **Click on the Close button to close the print preview screen.**

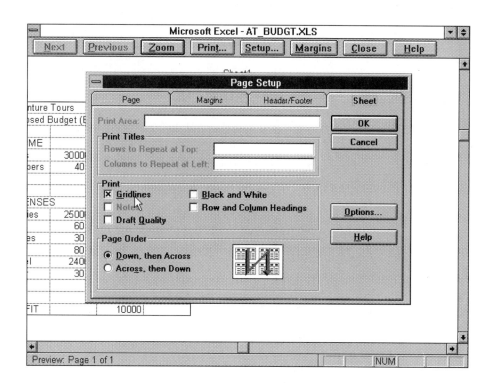

CLOSING A WORKSHEET

To close a worksheet, you must close the workbook that contains the worksheet. When you have finished working with a worksheet, you can use the **Close command** from the File menu to close it. If you have not saved the document, or if you have changed the document and not saved the changes, a message will appear when you try to close the document window. To illustrate this, you will make a change to the at_budgt document and then try to close it.

1. **Change the salaries expense to 220000.**

2. **Click on File in the menu bar.**

3. **Click on Close.**

The message Save changes in 'AT_BUDGT.XLS'? appears.

4. **Click on Yes.**

The changed document replaces the previously saved document, and the workbook window is removed from the screen. If there are no more open documents, only two menu options, File and Help, appear in the menu bar. To work with another document, you must open a new (blank) worksheet or open a previously saved document.

OPENING A WORKSHEET

The **Open command** from the File menu is used to open a previously saved document. As with the Save command, you must indicate the disk drive and file name when opening a file. Complete the following steps to open at_budgt.xls:

1. **Click on File in the menu bar.**

2. **Click on Open.**

The Open dialog box appears. This dialog box has several of the same parts as the Save As dialog box. A major difference is that the Open dialog box displays a list of files you can choose from to open. The files listed depends on the specified drive, directory, and file type. Figure 1.20 shows the drive as a, the directory as a:\, and the file type as Microsoft Excel Files (*.xl*). The *.xl* means any file with a file name extension that starts with .xl (such as .xls) will be displayed. Thus, the settings in Figure 1.20 cause all Excel files on the disk in drive A to be displayed in the File Name list box. Then you would choose a file from this list to open. Because the settings may be different in your dialog box, take a moment to display the list of drives.

3. **Point to the down arrow in the Drives list box (see Figure 1.20).**

4. **Click the mouse button.**

The list of drives appears, including drives a, b, and c. Choose the drive your data disk is located in.

5. **Click on a: (or b:).**

The File Name list box displays the Excel files on the disk in the selected drive. To open a file, click on the file name to highlight it and then click on OK.

6. **Point to at_budgt.xls.**

7. **Click the mouse button to select (highlight) it.**

1.20

Pointing to the down arrow in the Drives list box

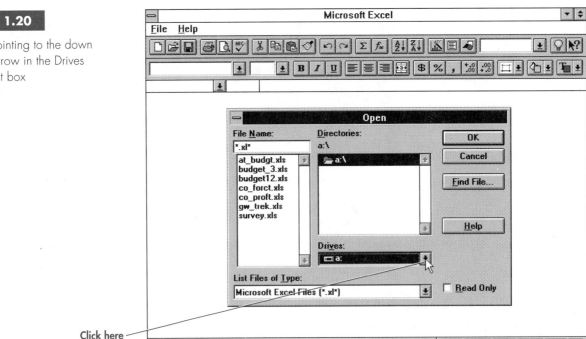

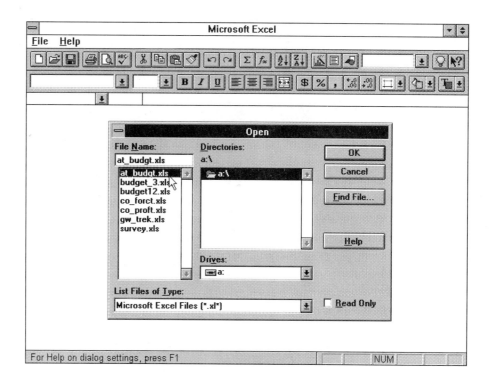

Your dialog box should resemble Figure 1.21.

8. Click on OK.

The at_budgt document is opened.

USING THE EXCEL TOOLBARS

Excel provides several tools that can be used as shortcuts when carrying out various Excel commands. Initially, two toolbars (Standard and Formatting) are displayed near the top of the workbook screen. Other toolbars, such as Chart and Drawing, can be displayed as needed. Figure 1.22 labels the following four commonly used tools on the Standard toolbar:

- New Workbook. Click on this button to open a new workbook and display a new worksheet.

- Open. Click on this button to display the Open dialog box, which allows you to open a previously saved file.

- Save. Click on this button to save the displayed workbook. If the document was previously saved, it is saved again with the same file name. If the document has not been previously saved, the Save As dialog box appears, allowing you to specify a drive and file name. Be careful with this tool. Often, you will create a document and save it. Then you will make changes in the document and decide to save both versions. If you use the Save tool to save the revised version, the same file name is used, and the first document is replaced by the second one.

New Workbook
Open
Save
Print

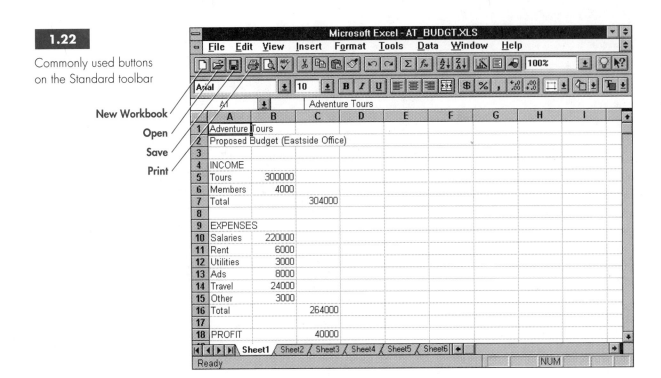

To save both documents, you would use the Save As command and give the second document a different file name.

■ Print. Click on this button to print the displayed document. Be careful with this tool. The Print dialog box does not appear, nor does the print preview screen. It is advisable to preview any document before printing it to make sure it will print the way you desire.

If you point to a button, its name will appear. Also, a description of the tool's function is displayed on the status line.

1. **Point to the Print button.**

2. **Read the description at the bottom of the screen.**

3. **On your own, point to the other buttons and read their descriptions.**

(*Note:* You may not understand the function of every tool. Many of them are explained in later chapters.)

FORMATTING CELLS

Excel allows you to use special characters, including dollar signs, commas, and decimal places, when entering numbers. However, there are two considerations you need to understand. First, when you enter a number with decimal places, any zeros at the end of the number may not be displayed. For example, when you enter the number 4.50, it may appear in the cell as 4.5. This is because the zero has no significance in the value of the number. You can format the cell so that it will display two decimal places. Second, when you use these special

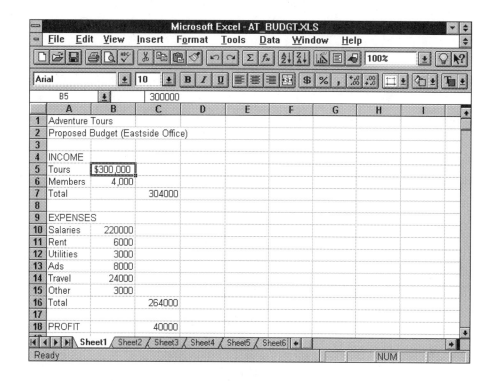

characters, you may find that the number is too large to fit within the cell width. In this section you learn how to enter the special characters and format cells.

Figure 1.23 shows the document with a dollar sign and a comma displayed for the tours income ($300,000). And the members income is changed to 4,000. Duplicate these entries.

1. **Enter** $300,000 **into B5.**

Notice that the formula bar displays 300000, the number without the dollar sign and comma.

2. **Enter** 4,000 **into B6.**

You could continue to change the other entries to display commas, or you could use the style tools on the Formatting toolbar to change all the numbers at one time. To do so, you select the numbers and click on the desired style.

$ Currency Style. This style displays a $, commas, and two decimal places

% Percent Style. This style multiplies the number by 100 and displays a % sign.

, Comma Style. This style formats the cell(s) to display commas and two decimal places.

Increase Decimal. Click on this button to format the cell to display one decimal place. Click on it again to display two decimal places.

Decrease Decimal. Click on this button to reduce the number of decimal places displayed by one. Click again to decrease the decimal places displayed by two.

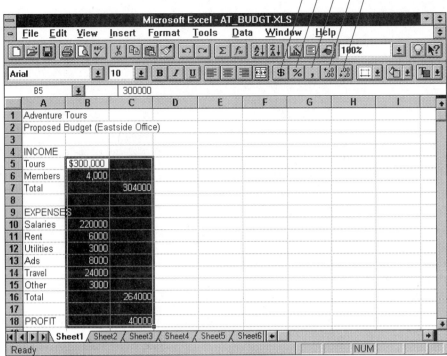

1.24

Style tools on the
Formatting toolbar

Take a moment to see how the Comma and Currency styles change the display of the numbers.

3. **Select cells B5 through C18.**

4. **Click on the Comma Style button (see Figure 1.24).**

Commas and two decimal places are inserted in the numbers. Notice that some of the cells display # signs. This indicates that the entry is too large for the cell width.

5. **Click on the Decrease Decimal button two times.**

No decimal places are displayed, and all the numbers now fit within the cell widths.

6. **Click on the Currency Style button.**

7. **Click on the Decrease Decimal button two times.**

Dollar signs, commas, and no decimal places appear. Again, some of the cells display # signs. Return to the Comma style.

8. **Choose the Comma style.**

CHANGING COLUMN WIDTHS

To remove the # signs so that the numbers will appear, you must increase the column widths. This can be done by choosing the Width command under Column in the Format menu or by using the mouse pointer to drag the column lines. You will use both methods. With the cells still selected:

1. **Click on Format in the menu bar.**

2. **Click on Column.**

Several options appear, including Width and AutoFit Selection. Choosing Width allows you to type a number (8.43 characters is the standard width) for the column width. Choosing AutoFit Selection will cause Excel to automatically adjust the column width to the longest entry in the column.

3. **Click on AutoFit Selection.**

The # signs are removed and the numbers displayed. Now use the drag method to increase the width for column A.

4. **Point to the line between the A and B column headings (see Figure 1.25). Notice that the pointer changes to a double arrow.**

5. **Hold down the mouse button, and drag the line to the right of the word *Tours* in row 1.**

6. **Release the mouse button.**

1.25

Pointing to the line between the A and B column headings

Point here

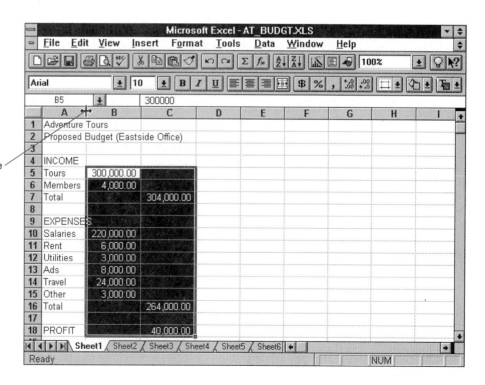

Now save the document using a different name and print it.

7. **Choose Save <u>A</u>s from the File menu.**

8. **Type** a:atbudgt2 (**or** b:atbudgt2).

9. **Click on OK.**

10. **Print the document.**

USING EXCEL HELP

If you need help while using the Excel program, you can use Excel's built-in Help function. There are several ways to use the **Help feature**, including viewing examples and demos, choosing topics from a Help index, and searching for a specific topic. The Search for Help on command in the Help menu opens a dialog box where you can request information on specific topics, such as printing or saving a document. When using the Search for Help on command, it is important to remember that information will probably be listed under key terms and command names rather than a related word. For instance, if you want to find information on formatting a number, you would use more specific terms such as *styles, comma,* or *currency,* but not a general word like *enhancing.* Key terms and command names will help you find information more quickly when using the Help feature. In this section you will learn the basics of the Help function.

1. **Click on <u>H</u>elp in the menu bar.**

2. **Click on <u>S</u>earch for Help on.**

The Help screen opens and the Search dialog box appears.

3. **Type** currency

Notice that as you type, the list box displays topics that relate to what you are typing; currency formats is the highlighted option.

4. **Verify that currency formats is selected.**

5. **Click on the <u>S</u>how Topics button.**

Four topics appear in the Select a topic box. Choose the topic called Formatting numbers with toolbar buttons.

6. **Click on Formatting numbers with toolbar buttons.**

7. **Click on <u>G</u>o To.**

The How To screen appears with information on the topic you selected from the list. You can scroll through the screen to view this information. You can also print the information, bring up the Help Index, or close the How To screen. Notice in the How To screen that some of the words are in a different color. You can click on these words, or jump terms, to display more information relating to that word or topic.

8. Scroll to locate the phrase **Comma Style Button**.

9. Click on **Comma Style Button**.

The Microsoft Excel Help screen comes to the top and displays information on the Comma Style button, including what chapter in the *User's Guide* provides information relating to this command. Also, across the top of this screen are several option buttons including:

- Contents. This button displays the main Excel Help screen you are now viewing.

- Search. This button brings up the Search dialog box.

- Back. This button takes you to the previously disaplayed screen within Excel Help.

- History. This button displays a list of the screens that you have viewed.

- Index. This button displays the Help index.

Now use the History button to show the screens you have displayed.

10. Click on **History**.

A window appears showing the screens that you have viewed. At this point, you could double-click on any of the items in the Windows Help History window to display the item. To close the window, choose Close from the control-menu box.

11. Click on the control-menu box for the Windows Help History window (see Figure 1.26).

12. Choose **Close** from the menu that appears.

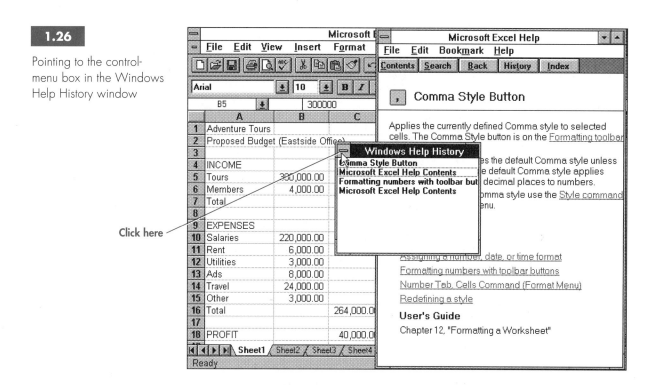

1.26

Pointing to the control-menu box in the Windows Help History window

Click here

Now close Excel Help using the control-menu box in the Help window.

13. **Click on the control-menu box in the Microsoft Excel Help window.**

14. **Click on Close.**

The How To screen reappears. Choose the Close button to remove it from the screen.

15. **Click on Close.**

The worksheet is displayed. You can also use the F1 key to access the Help feature. This is especially useful if you are in the middle of a process and need help completing it. Further, many of the dialog boxes have a Help button that can be used to get information on how to use the dialog box.

EXITING THE EXCEL PROGRAM

Before exiting Excel it is a good idea to close all open document windows.

1. **Choose Close from the File menu to close the atbudgt2 document.**

After closing all document windows, the application window is still displayed. However, only two options, File and Help, appear on the menu bar. There are two methods to exit Excel. You can choose Exit from the File menu, or you can choose Close from the control-menu box.

2. **Choose Exit from the File menu.**

When you are done using the computer, be sure to remove your data disk from the disk drive.

CHAPTER REVIEW

KEY TERMS

active cell	formula bar	row headings
Autosum	functions	Save As command
Book1	Help feature	Save command
cell	maximize button	scroll bars
Close command	menu bar	sheet tabs
column headings	Microsoft Excel 5.0	spreadsheet program
commands	Microsoft Windows	Standard toolbar
control-menu box	minimize button	status bar
document	mouse pointer	subdirectory
drive	Open command	SUM function
file	Print command	title bar
file name	reference bar	workbook
Formatting toolbar	restore button	worksheet

REVIEW QUESTIONS

1. **T F** An Excel worksheet is also called a document.

2. Where a row and a column intersect is called a _____.

3. The [Home] key selects column _____.

4. Formulas begin with an _____ _____.

5. **T F** Text entries must fit within the cell width to be displayed properly.

6. Numbers that are too large to fit in a cell will display in scientific notation or as a series of _____.

7. The _____ tool can be used as a shortcut for summing a group of numbers.

8. When saving a document, Excel automatically appends the extension _____ to the file name.

9. **T F** It is a good idea to preview a document before printing it.

10. **T F** The control-menu box can be used to exit the Excel program.

PROJECTS

1. Complete the worksheet, Income Forecast, shown in Figure 1.1. Use formulas for all calculations. Use the style buttons to format the first number to display a dollar sign and all the other numbers to display commas. Include your name at the bottom of the document. Save the workbook as ch1_p1, and then print the document.

2. Complete the worksheet, Survey Results, shown in Figure 1.1. Use the SUM function or the AutoSum tool for all calculations. Include your name at the bottom of the document. Save the workbook as ch1_p2, and then print the document.

3. Adventure Tours will be having a grand opening of their new Eastside office. A breakdown of the costs for the event follows. Create a worksheet showing these costs and include a total. Format the numbers to display commas and two decimal places. Format the total to display a dollar sign. Include your name at the bottom of the document. Save the workbook as ch1_p3, and then print the document.

Publicity	100
Food	500
Drinks	300
Banner	75
Invitations	150
Mailing	300
Door Prize	1,000
Misc.	200

4. Develop a college or household budget of your own. Use formulas and functions for all calculations. Include your name at the bottom of the document. Save the workbook as ch1_p4, and then print the document.

5. Using the Excel Help feature, answer the following:

   a. When you search for the word *printing*, what are some of the print-related topics displayed in the Search dialog box?

   b. What is the process for exiting the Help feature?

2

Developing and Analyzing a Worksheet

Excel provides several shortcuts for entering data in a worksheet. These include copying and moving data as well as filling in a group of cells with series data such as a series of months. Figure 2.1 shows an Adventure Tours six-month projected budget for the Eastside office. You will develop this worksheet using several shortcuts for entering the numbers and headings.

2.1

A six-month projected budget

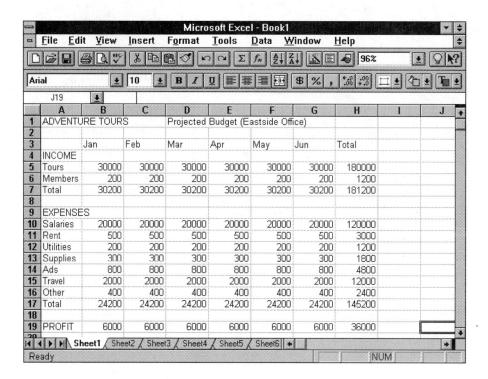

ENTERING A SERIES OF DATES

Start with a blank worksheet.

1. **Start Excel.**

Excel **Fill commands** allow you to quickly enter a series of dates (Jan, Feb, Mar, and so on) by typing the first date and then using the mouse pointer to select the cells that will contain the other dates. Complete the following steps to enter the dates. Start by entering the heading into cell A1.

2. **With cell A1 selected, type** ADVENTURE TOURS

3. **Select cell D1.**

4. **Type** Projected Budget (Eastside Office)

5. **Select cell B3.**

6. **Type** Jan

7. **Click on the enter box on the formula bar.**

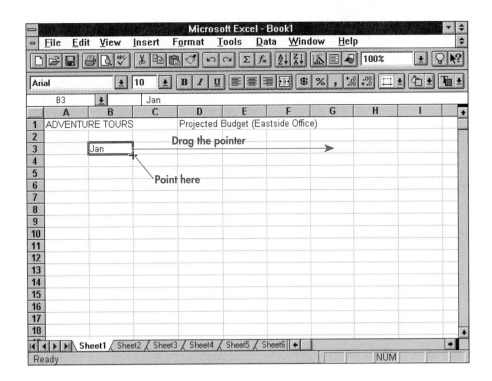

Figure 2.2 shows the process for entering the other dates. You point to the handle at the lower-right corner of cell B3. The pointer changes to a crosshair. Then you hold down the mouse button and drag the pointer to select the other cells (C3 through G3). Finally, you release the mouse button, and the dates are automatically entered into the selected cells. This process is called **drag and drop**.

   8. Point to the handle at the lower-right corner of cell B3.

   9. When the pointer changes to a crosshair, hold down the mouse button and drag the pointer to select cells C3 through G3.

   10. Release the mouse button.

The other months are entered into the selected cells. This same process can be used to enter a series of days (Mon, Tue, Wed, . . .) and years (1995, 1996, 1997, . . .). (*Note:* When working with years, you need to type an apostrophe (') before the date so the entry is not considered a number.) The Series command under Fill in the Edit menu can also be used to enter a series of dates as well as a series of numbers.

Now continue by entering the headings in column A and the numbers in column B as shown in Figure 2.3.

   11. On your own, enter the headings in column A and the numbers in column B.

Your worksheet should resemble Figure 2.3.

2.3

The headings in column
A and the numbers in
column B

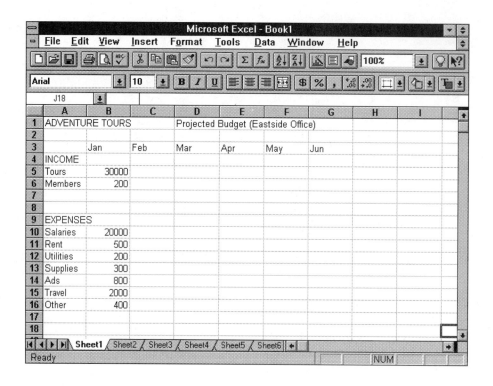

COPYING WORKSHEET DATA

Notice in Figure 2.1 that the numbers in this budget are the same for each month. You can enter the numbers for January and then use Excel's copy feature to quickly enter the numbers for the other months. There are three methods used to copy data within a worksheet: the **Copy** and **Paste commands** from the Edit menu, the Fill command from the Edit menu, and the drag-and-drop process using the mouse. We will use each of these methods to copy the budget numbers from January to the other months. Start by using the copy-and-paste method to copy the tour income from cell B5 to cells C5 through G5.

1. **Select cell B5.**

2. **Point to <u>E</u>dit in the menu bar.**

3. **Click the mouse button.**

4. **Click on <u>C</u>opy.**

The entry (30000) in cell B5 is placed into a holding area called the **Clipboard**. Notice that a moving border, called a marquee, surrounds cell B5. This indicates which data has been placed on the Clipboard.

5. **Select cell C5.**

6. **Click on <u>E</u>dit in the menu bar.**

7. **Click on <u>P</u>aste.**

The number (30000) is copied from the Clipboard to the selected cell. The number is still on the Clipboard and can be copied to other cells.

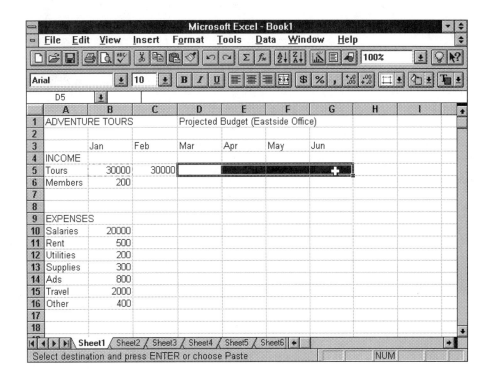

8. Point to D5.

9. Hold down the mouse button and drag the pointer to select cells D5 through G5 (see Figure 2.4).

10. Release the mouse button.

11. Click on **Paste** in the Edit menu.

The number (30000) is copied from the Clipboard to the selected cells. To remove the marquee, press the (Esc) key.

12. Press (Esc).

Now use the copy-and-paste method to copy the members income (200) from cell B6 to cells C6 through G6.

13. On your own, copy the members income.

14. When done, remove the marquee.

Next you will use the Fill command to copy the salaries (20000) from cell B10 to cells C10 through G10. The process is to select the cell to be copied and the cells to be copied to, and then choose Fill from the Edit menu and select Right from the list of commands.

15. Select cells B10 through G10.

16. Click on **Edit** in the menu bar.

17. Click on **Fill**.

18. Click on **Right**.

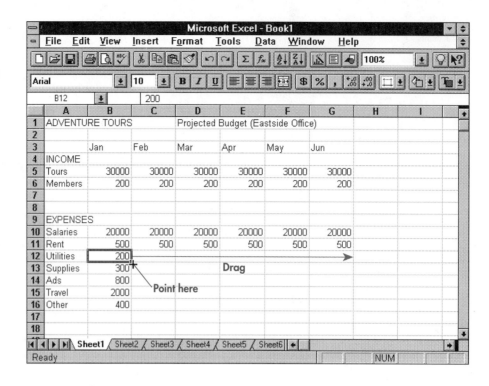

The number (20000) is copied to the selected cells. Now use the Fill command to copy the rent expense (500).

19. **On your own, copy the rent expense in row 11.**

Next use the drag-and-drop method to copy the utilities expense.

20. **Select cell B12.**

21. **Point to the handle at the lower-right corner of cell B12.**

22. **When the pointer changes to a crosshair, hold down the mouse button and drag the pointer to select cells C12 through G12 (see Figure 2.5).**

23. **Release the mouse button.**

The number (200) is copied to the selected cells.

24. **On your own, use the drag-and-drop method to copy the supplies expense.**

Until now you have been copying one cell at a time. You can copy more than one cell using any of the three methods. Use the drag-and-drop method to copy the remaining entries.

25. **Select cells B14 through B16.**

26. **Point to the handle at the lower-right corner of cell B16.**

27. **When the pointer changes to a crosshair, hold down the mouse button and drag the pointer to select cells C14 through G16 (see Figure 2.6).**

28. **Release the mouse button.**

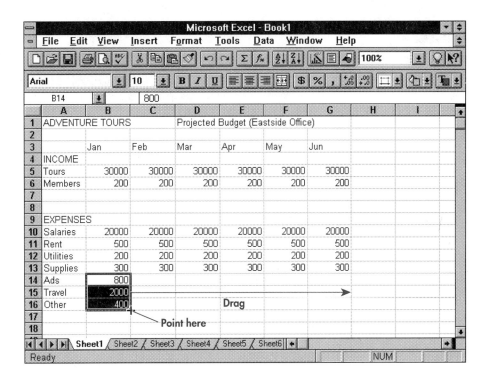

The numeric entries are completed. Which of the three copying methods you
use may depend on where you are copying to. The Fill commands are used to
copy data from a cell(s) to an adjacent cell(s). The other two methods can be
used when you are not copying to adjacent cells. To illustrate this, you will use
the drag-and-drop method to copy the word *Total* from cell A7 to A17.
Because you will not be copying to adjacent cells, you will need to use the Ctrl
key to perform this operation.

29. **Select cell A7.**

30. **Type** Total

31. **Click on the enter box on the formula bar.**

32. **Point to the border of the cell (not the handle).**

33. **Hold down** Ctrl.

Notice that a small crosshair appears next to the pointer (see Figure 2.7). This
indicates that you will be copying data.

34. **Hold down the mouse button and drag the pointer to cell A17.**

35. **Release the mouse button.**

36. **Release** Ctrl.

The word *Total* is copied to cell A17.

37. **On your own, use the drag-and-drop method to copy the word** *Total*
to cell H3.

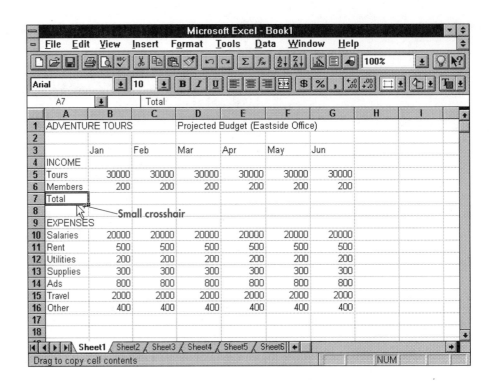

COPYING FORMULAS AND FUNCTIONS

Any of the three copying methods can be used to copy formulas and functions. Figure 2.8 shows the formulas that are to be entered to display the income totals for each month. Notice that the formulas are the same except that the cell references change relative to the column. That is, =B5+B6 for column B and =C5+C6 for column C. When you copy a formula, Excel automatically changes the cell references relative to the new location. To illustrate this, you will enter the formula for column B and then copy it to the other columns.

1. Select cell B7.

2. Type =B5+B6

3. Click on the enter box on the formula bar.

4. Point to the handle at the lower-right corner of cell B7.

5. When the pointer changes to a crosshair, hold down the mouse button and drag the pointer to cell G7.

6. Release the mouse button.

7. Select cell C7.

Notice that the formula bar displays =C5+C6. Now complete the total rows for the expenses and profit.

8. Select cell B17.

9. Click on the AutoSum button.

10. Click on the enter box on the formula bar.

11. On your own, copy the function across the row.

2.8

The formulas for row 7

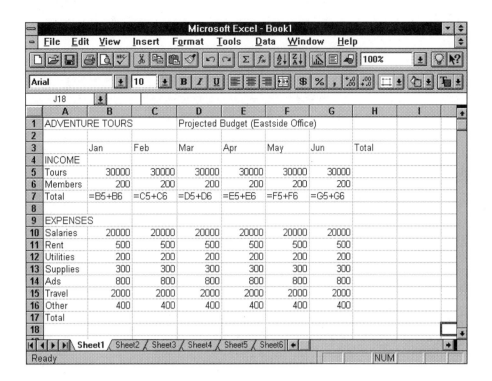

12. **Enter** PROFIT **into cell A19.**

13. **Select cell B19.**

14. **Type** =B7–B17

15. **Click on the enter box on the formula bar.**

16. **On your own, copy the formula across the row.**

Now complete the total column (column H).

17. **Select cell H5.**

18. **Use the AutoSum button to enter the SUM function.**

19. **Use the drag-and-drop method to copy the function to cells H6 and H7.**

20. **On your own, total the salaries row.**

21. **On your own, copy the formula to total the other expense categories.**

22. **On your own, total the profit row.**

Your worksheet should resemble Figure 2.1.

WORKING WITH
ABSOLUTE CELL REFERENCES

As we mentioned earlier, when you copy a formula the cell references change relative to the formula's new location. This may not be desirable. Study Figure 2.9, which shows the percentage each expense category is of the total expenses. For example, salaries are budgeted at 82.64 percent of total expenses

2.9

The percentage each
expense category is of
the total expenses

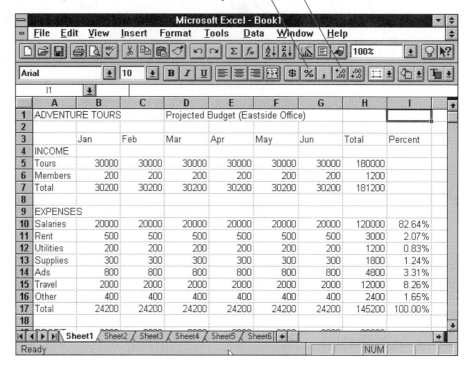

and ads at 3.31 percent. Figure 2.10 shows the formulas used to calculate these percentages. Notice that a part of the formula, H17, the total expenses, remains the same for all the formulas. This is because total expenses is divided into each expense category. Therefore, when copying the formula, you do not want Excel to change H17. This is done by typing $H$17 so that Excel treats the cell as an **absolute cell reference**, that is, one that does not change when the formula is copied.

1. **Enter** Percent **into I3.**

2. **Select cell I10.**

3. **Type =H10/$H$17**

4. **Click on the enter box on the formula bar.**

Notice that the result is displayed as a decimal, 0.826446. Later you will learn how to change the display to a percent.

5. **Copy the formula through I17.**

6. **Select cell I5.**

7. **Type =H5/$H$7**

8. **Click on the enter box on the formula bar.**

9. **Copy the formula through I7.**

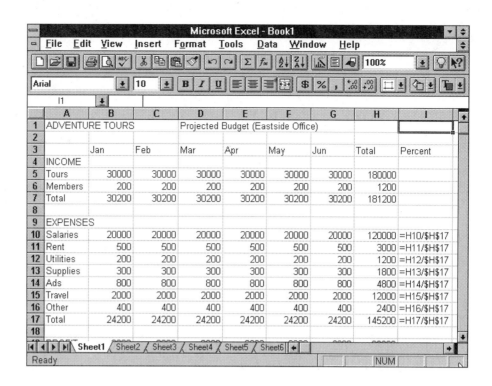

FORMATTING ENTRIES AS PERCENTS

The formulas you have just entered display the results as decimals rather than percents. If nothing else was done to the worksheet, the percent column could be misleading or at least confusing. For example, the salaries number would be read as .826446 percent. That is, less than 1 percent. The number should read 82.6446 percent. There are two ways to correct the display. First you could change the formula by multiplying it by 100 (=H10/$H$17*100). Second you could format the entry to display in **percent format**. When you format an entry to display as a percent, Excel multiplies the entry by 100 and enters a percent sign (%). Figure 2.9 shows the results of formatting the percent column. The process is to select the numbers to be formatted and select the desired style button on the Formatting toolbar.

1. **Select cells I10 through I17.**

2. **Click on the Percent Style button on the Formatting toolbar (see Figure 2.9).**

3. **Click twice on the Increase Decimal button (see Figure 2.9).**

The numbers are displayed as percents with two decimal places. It is important to understand that the value of the number has not changed, only how the number is displayed in the worksheet. Now format the other numbers.

4. **Select cells I5 through I7.**

5. **On your own, format the cells to display percents with two decimal places.**

MOVING WORKSHEET DATA

Excel provides two methods to move worksheet data, cut-and-paste and drag-and-drop. The cut-and-paste process is similar to the copy-and-paste process. You select the desired data to move and choose the **Cut command** from the Edit menu. The data is removed from the worksheet and placed on the Clipboard. Then you select the location to move the data to and choose Paste from the Edit menu. The drag-and-drop process involves pointing to the border of the selected cell or cell range and dragging the pointer to the desired location. Use the drag-and-drop method to move the words *Projected Budget (Eastside Office)* to cell A2. (*Note:* To select the words, you do not need to select all the cells that the words appear in, only the cell the words are entered in.)

1. **Click on cell D1.**

2. **Point to the border (not the handle) of D1 (see Figure 2.11).**

3. **Hold down the mouse button and drag the pointer to cell A2. Notice the box that moves along with the pointer.**

4. **Release the mouse button.**

The words are moved to cell A2. Now save and print the worksheet.

5. **Save the worksheet as bdgt_6mo.**

6. **Print the worksheet.**

2.11

Pointing to the cell border to move an entry

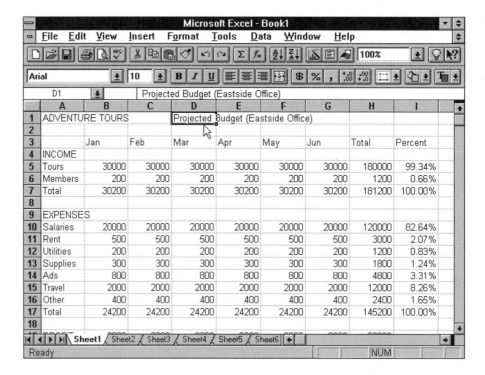

PERFORMING WHAT-IF ANALYSIS

The budget you have just developed forecasts Adventure Tours's profit for the next six months. If their income and expenditure projections are accurate, they will generate $36,000 in profits. However, the budget is based on the assumption that income and expenses will remain constant throughout the six months. This may be true for some items such as rent, but it is reasonable to assume that most items will vary. For example, income in June may be higher than the other months because more travel is done in the summer. Therefore, the budget is best used as a model to perform **what-if analysis**, which can show what will happen under different assumptions (that is, what if a change is made in the notebook?). For example, what would happen if income doubled in June or advertising expenses increased by 10 percent in May? Because formulas have been used to establish relationships among cells, the results of any changes you make are immediately displayed. Complete the following what-if scenarios, and note the effect on overall profits.

What would happen if tours income doubled in June?

1. **Enter** 60000 **into cell G5.**

What would happen if advertising expenses increased by 10 percent in May?

2. **Enter** 880 **into cell F14.**

What if salaries increased by 10 percent in June? This time use a formula to calculate the new number. Take the value in F10 (May salaries) and multiply it by 110 percent.

3. **Select cell G10.**

4. **Type** =F10*110%

5. **Press** ⏎Enter.

Each individual change you have made recalculates the profit.

You could continue to make individual changes in the worksheet, or you could make several changes at one time. For example, say Adventure Tours wants to know the result of increasing sales by 5 percent each month. One process for calculating this increase is to enter a formula for February and copy the formula for the other months. The formula for February would be the January number multiplied by 105 percent, the formula for March would be the February number multiplied by 105 percent, and so forth.

6. **Select cell C5.**

7. **Type** =B5*105%

8. **Click on the enter box on the formula bar.**

Now copy this formula to March through June.

9. **Drag the handle to copy cell C5 to cells D5 through G5.**

10. **Click on D5.**

Notice that the entry in the formula bar is =C5*105%. Each month there is a 5 percent increase in tours income over the previous month. Now any change in one month will be reflected in the subsequent months. Change January tours income to 40000.

11. Enter 40000 into cell B5.

All the months are increased accordingly. Instead of a percentage increase each month, Adventure Tours may decide that they would like to know the result of increasing income by a fixed amount (1000) each month. Again, a formula could be entered and then copied. The formula for February would be the January amount plus 1000.

12. Select cell C5.

13. Type =B5+1000

14. Click on the enter box on the formula bar.

15. Copy the formula to the other months.

Now assume that Adventure Tours wants to see the results of increasing the members income by 10 percent each month.

16. On your own, enter and copy the formula to calculate the members income based on a 10% increase each month.

Next assume that Adventure Tours wants to see the results of increasing the members income by $50 each month.

17. On your own, enter and copy the formula to calculate the members income based on a $50 increase each month.

INSERTING ROWS AND COLUMNS

Excel allows you to insert blank rows and columns to make room for additional data. Figure 2.12 shows a new expense category inserted at row 16 and a new month inserted at column H. The process is to select the row or column and use the **Rows** or **Columns command** from the Insert menu. Complete the following steps to duplicate Figure 2.12:

1. Click on row heading 16 to select (highlight) the row.

2. Click on Insert in the menu bar.

3. Click on Rows.

A blank row is inserted at row 16. The data in row 16 moves to row 17, the data in row 17 moves to row 18, and so forth.

4. Click on column heading H to select the column.

5. Choose Columns from the Insert menu.

A blank column is inserted at column H. Now complete the entries.

2.12

The notebook after inserting a new row at 16 and a new column at H

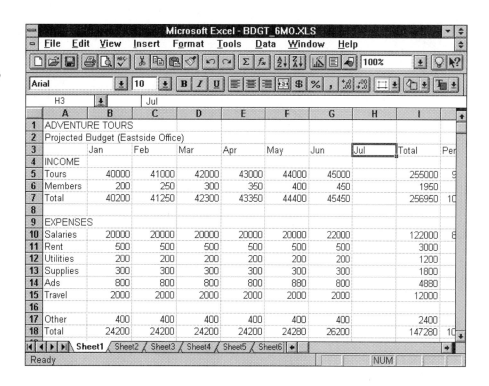

6. Enter Jul into cell **H3**.

7. Select cells **G5** through **H20**.

8. Choose F**ill** from the Edit menu.

9. Choose **Right** from the list of commands.

10. Enter Printing into cell **A16**.

11. Enter 125 into cell **B16**.

12. Copy 125 to the other months.

Because you have inserted a column (H) outside the range used to calculate the totals (B–G), you will need to reenter the function for the total column.

13. Select **I5**.

14. Use the AutoSum button to recalculate the total tours income.

15. Copy the function to total the other rows.

16. On your own, complete the percent for the printing expense category.

Your document should resemble Figure 2.13.

17. Save the document as bdgt_7mo.

18. Print the document. (*Note:* The document will print on two pages.)

19. Close the document window.

This completes the section on inserting rows and columns.

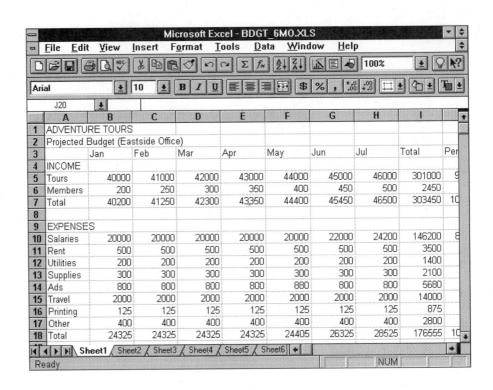

	A	B	C	D	E	F	G	H	I	Per
1	ADVENTURE TOURS									
2	Projected Budget (Eastside Office)									
3		Jan	Feb	Mar	Apr	May	Jun	Jul	Total	Per
4	INCOME									
5	Tours	40000	41000	42000	43000	44000	45000	46000	301000	9
6	Members	200	250	300	350	400	450	500	2450	
7	Total	40200	41250	42300	43350	44400	45450	46500	303450	10
8										
9	EXPENSES									
10	Salaries	20000	20000	20000	20000	20000	22000	24200	146200	8
11	Rent	500	500	500	500	500	500	500	3500	
12	Utilities	200	200	200	200	200	200	200	1400	
13	Supplies	300	300	300	300	300	300	300	2100	
14	Ads	800	800	800	800	880	800	800	5680	
15	Travel	2000	2000	2000	2000	2000	2000	2000	14000	
16	Printing	125	125	125	125	125	125	125	875	
17	Other	400	400	400	400	400	400	400	2800	
18	Total	24325	24325	24325	24325	24405	26325	28525	176555	10

CHAPTER REVIEW

KEY TERMS

absolute cell reference
Clipboard
Columns command
Copy command

Cut command
drag and drop
Fill commands
Paste command

percent format
Rows command
what-if analysis

REVIEW QUESTIONS

1. **T F** The drag-and-drop method can be used to enter a series of dates.

2. **T F** The Copy and Paste commands and the Fill commands are two methods used to copy data in a worksheet.

3. When using the drag-and-drop method to copy data, you point to the _____ corner of the cell.

4. A cell reference that does not change when a formula is copied is called a(n) _____ cell reference.

5. **T F** Formatting a number to display a percent sign automatically multiplies the number by 100.

6. When using the drag-and-drop method to move data, you point to the cell _____.

7. **T F**   Inserting rows and columns is done with the Rows and Columns commands from the Insert menu.

PROJECTS

1. Adventure Tours wants to log the number of phone calls per hour for one week. This will help them decide on whether or not they need a new phone system. Use Excel to develop the following form. (*Hint:* Use the drag-and-drop process to enter the column heading for the days.) Use the SUM function or the AutoSum button to enter the total once, and then copy the formulas to the other cells. Include your name at the bottom of the document. Save the workbook as ch2_p1. Print the document with gridlines and row and column headings.

PHONE CALLS RECEIVED:

	Mon	Tue	Wed	Thu	Fri	Sat	Total	
9:00								0
10:00								0
11:00								0
12:00								0
1:00								0
2:00								0
3:00								0
4:00								0
Total	0	0	0	0	0	0	0	0

2. Adventure Tours will be installing a computerized tour information system called Computour. This system will use compact disks to provide electronic brochures of various tours. The monthly fee for updating the CDs is $100. Using the bdgt_6mo worksheet, insert a row above the travel expense category and enter a new category, Computour. Enter 100 for January, and copy the entry for the other months. Complete the total column. Increase the column width for column A so that Computour fits. Use the drag-and-drop method to move the heading, *ADVENTURE TOURS*, to column C and to move the subheading, *Projected Budget (Eastside Office)*, to column F. Include your name at the bottom of the document. Save the workbook as ch2_p2. Print the document with gridlines and row and column headings.

3. Following is the projected budget for Adventure Tours's downtown office. Develop a worksheet using this information. Use the drag-and-drop process for entering the month headings and the various copy processes for entering the

numbers. Complete the total and profit rows and the total and percent columns on your own. Use formulas and functions for all calculations. Include your name at the bottom of the document. Save the worksheet as ch2_p3. Print the document with gridlines and row and column headings.

ADVENTURE TOURS

Projected Budget (Downtown Office)

	Jan	Feb	Mar	Apr	May	Jun	Total	Percent
INCOME								
Tours	40000	40000	40000	40000	40000	40000		
Members	250	250	250	250	250	250		
Total								
EXPENSES								
Salaries	30000	30000	30000	30000	30000	30000		
Rent	600	600	600	600	600	600		
Utilities	220	220	220	220	220	220		
Supplies	400	400	400	400	400	400		
Ads	1000	1000	1000	1000	1000	1000		
Travel	2500	2500	2500	2500	2500	2500		
Other	400	400	400	400	400	400		
Total								
PROFIT								

4. Following is an analysis of the actual and forecasted income, expenses, and profit for 1995. Duplicate this worksheet. The % difference column is calculated by dividing the difference by the actual amount. Format the percents to display two decimal places. Use formulas and functions for all calculations. Include your name at the bottom of the document. Save the workbook as ch2_p4. Print the document with gridlines and row and column headings.

COMPARISON OF ACTUAL AND FORECASTED NUMBERS FOR 1995

	1995 (Actual)	1995 (Forecast)	Difference (Act-For)	% Difference
Income	450,000	400,000	50,000	11.11%
Expenses	420,000	375,000	45,000	10.71%
Profit	30,000	25,000	5,000	16.67%

5. Using the Quick Preview command in the Help menu, review the concepts you learned in Chapters 1 and 2. When the Quick Preview screen appears, choose the Getting Started option. (*Note:* Check with your instructor or lab assistant to see whether this Help feature has been installed on your machine.)

3

Enhancing a Worksheet

This chapter shows you how to make changes in the worksheet to enhance its appearance. Excel allows you to make several types of changes to make a document easier to read and more interesting to view, as well as draw the reader's attention to specific parts of the document. Figure 3.1 shows the Adventure Tours budget after the following changes have been made:

- The heading *ADVENTURE TOURS* has been centered across the worksheet and changed to a different font and size.

- The letters *A* and *T* in the heading have been changed to a larger font size.

- The subheading *Projected Budget (Eastside Office)* has been centered across the worksheet and formatted in italic type.

- The column headings have been right aligned within the cells.

- The words *Total* are centered in the cells.

- The worksheet, except for the text box and arrow, has a single-line border around it.

- The column headings have a double-line border around them.

- The overall profit has a thick border around it.

- The total rows have a single line above them.

- The profit row has a double-line above it.

- The column headings have a dotted pattern within the border.

3.1

The enhanced document

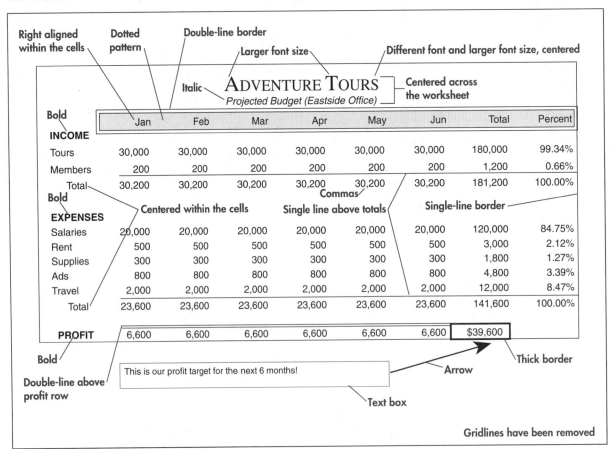

E 56

- The words *INCOME*, *EXPENSES*, and *PROFIT* are in bold type.
- The numbers are formatted to display commas.
- There is a text box with a sentence typed inside it.
- There is an arrow from the text box to the overall profit number.
- The gridlines have been removed from the worksheet.

ALIGNING DATA IN THE WORKSHEET

Start by opening a budget workbook called budget_6. This workbook is similar to the one you created in Chapter 2.

1. **Start Excel.**

2. **Open budget_6.xls.**

Excel allows you to **align data** within cells and across cells. Data can be right, left, or center aligned within a cell and center aligned across cells. The default setting for text entries is left aligned, and the default setting for numeric entries is right aligned. You can change the alignment by selecting the desired cells and choosing one of the alignment buttons on the Formatting toolbar (see Figure 3.2).

Figure 3.2 shows the heading and subheading centered across the worksheet. To center an entry across cells, you select all the cells and then choose the **Center Across Columns button** (see Figure 3.2). In this case you will center the words *ADVENTURE TOURS* across cells A1 through I1.

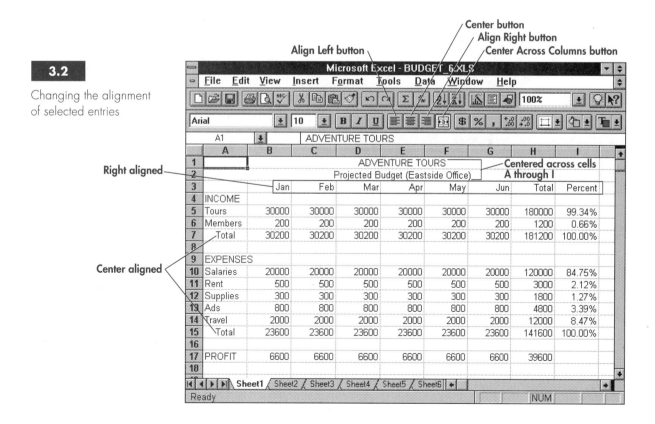

3.2

Changing the alignment of selected entries

3. Select cells A1 through I1.

4. Click on the Center Across Columns button.

It is important to understand that *ADVENTURE TOURS* is still in cell A1. It only displays in the other cells. To illustrate this, select cell D1.

5. Click on D1.

Notice that the formula bar is empty, indicating there is no entry in this cell.

6. Click on A1.

Notice that the formula bar displays *ADVENTURE TOURS*.

7. On your own, center *Projected Budget (Eastside Office)* across the worksheet.

Next you will right-align the column headings. Start by aligning the *Jan* heading.

8. Select cell B3.

9. Click on the Align Right button on the Formatting toolbar.

Notice how the heading *Jan* is aligned to the right of the cell. Now right-align the other headings.

10. Select C3 through I3.

11. Click on the Align Right button.

Now center (within the cell, not across cells) the word *Total*.

12. Select A7.

13. Click on the Center alignment button.

14. On your own, center-align the word *Total* in cell A15.

This completes the section on aligning data. Remember, you can center-align data across several cells, and you can center, right-align, and left-align data within a cell. You can align numbers as well as text.

WORKING WITH BORDERS AND LINES

Excel allows you to format any cell or cells to display borders or lines. Figure 3.3 shows the use of several types of borders, which we describe here:

- Single-line border completely surrounding the worksheet

- Double-line border around the column headings

- Thick-line border around the overall profits

- Single lines above the total rows

- Double line above the profit row

These **borders** (or outlines) and **lines** are created using the Format Cells dialog box from the Format menu. Before duplicating Figure 3.3, you need to turn off

ADVENTURE TOURS
Projected Budget (Eastside Office)

Single-line border

Double-line border

Single lines

	Jan	Feb	Mar	Apr	May	Jun	Total	Percent
INCOME								
Tours	30000	30000	30000	30000	30000	30000	180000	99.34%
Members	200	200	200	200	200	200	1200	0.66%
Total	30200	30200	30200	30200	30200	30200	181200	100.00%
EXPENSES								
Salaries	20000	20000	20000	20000	20000	20000	120000	82.64%
Rent	500	500	500	500	500	500	3000	2.07%
Utilities	200	200	200	200	200	200	1200	0.83%
Supplies	300	300	300	300	300	300	1800	1.24%
Ads	800	800	800	800	800	800	4800	3.31%
Travel	2000	2000	2000	2000	2000	2000	12000	8.26%
Other	400	400	400	400	400	400	2400	1.65%
Total	24200	24200	24200	24200	24200	24200	145200	100.00%
PROFIT	6000	6000	6000	6000	6000	6000	36000	

Double line

Thick-line border

the display of the gridlines. This will make it easier for you to see the borders you create. This is done using the Options command from the Tools menu.

1. Click on <u>T</u>ools in the menu bar.

2. Click on <u>O</u>ptions.

The Options dialog box appears. This dialog box has several sections, each one labeled by a tab that looks like an index card. To see the options in a section of the dialog box, click on the tab for that section.

3. Click on the View tab. (*Note:* The View section of the dialog box may already be displayed. If so, it is unnecessary to click on the tab for that section.)

Several choices appear that affect what you see on the monitor. Each option that has an X beside it is turned on and will display on the monitor. For example, when the Row & Column Headers option is turned on, the row headings (1, 2, 3, . . .) and the column headings (A, B, C, . . .) will be displayed. You click on an option to turn it off and on.

4. Click on <u>G</u>ridlines under Window Options in the View section.

5. Click on OK.

The gridlines are removed from the display. It is important to understand that this affects only the display on the monitor and not the printout. To specify not to print gridlines, you use the Page Setup command in the File menu.

6. Click on File in the menu bar.

7. Click on Page Setup.

The Page Setup dialog box appears. In this dialog box there are also several sections marked with tabs. The Sheet section allows you to change certain aspects of the printed page, including whether or not gridlines appear.

8. Click on the Sheet tab to display this section of the dialog box.

9. If the Gridlines option has an X next to it, click on it to remove the X.

10. Click on OK.

Now insert the borders and lines. Start with the border around the entire worksheet. The first step is to select the cells.

11. Select cells A1 through I17.

12. Click on Format in the menu bar.

13. Click on Cells.

The Format Cells dialog box is displayed. The Border section allows you to specify the type of border lines and where they will appear.

14. Click on the Border tab.

The Outline option under Border places a border around the entire selected cell or cell range. The other options place a line at the left, right, top, or bottom of the selected cell or cell range. In the Style box you can choose from dotted, dashed, thin, thick, single, and double lines. Currently, the single thin line is selected as indicated by the darkened border around that style. You need to select Outline so a border will appear around the entire cell range (A1 through I19).

15. Click on Outline to select it.

Your screen should resemble Figure 3.4.

16. Click on OK.

The border is inserted in the worksheet. It is difficult to see the border because the cells are still highlighted.

17. Click on cell A1 to select it and remove the highlighting from the other cells.

Now preview the document to see how it will print. This time use the Print Preview button.

18. Click on the Print Preview button (see Figure 3.4).

The document appears with the border around the entire worksheet. Next insert a double-line border around the column headings.

19. Click on the Close button to return to the worksheet.

20. Select cells B3 through I3.

21. Choose Cells from the Format menu.

22. If necessary, click on the Border tab to display those options.

3.4

The completed Format
Cells dialog box to
insert a border around
the selected cells

Print Preview button

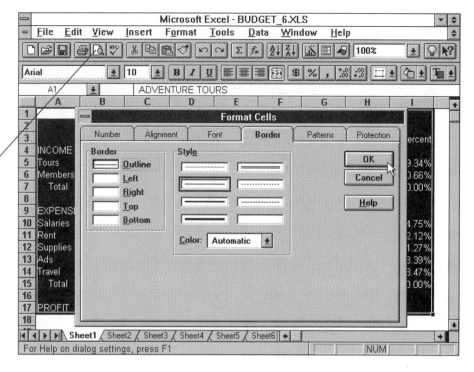

23. **Click on <u>O</u>utline to select it.**

24. **Click on the double-line style to select it.**

25. **Click on OK.**

26. **Preview the document.**

27. **Return to the worksheet.**

Next insert a thick-line border around the overall profit number in cell H17.

28. **On your own, insert a thick-line border around the overall profit number.** (*Hint:* **Choose the <u>O</u>utline option in the Border section of the Format Cells dialog box.)**

29. **Preview the document.**

The print preview screen should resemble Figure 3.5. Use the Zoom feature to view the profit number.

30. **Point to the profit number (see Figure 3.5).**

31. **Click the mouse button.**

The area surrounding the pointer is enlarged, and you can see the thick border.

32. **Click the mouse button to return to the original view.**

33. **Return to the worksheet.**

The last border lines you will insert are those above the total and profit rows. Notice (in Figure 3.3) that these are not outline borders but rather single or double lines that appear above the selected rows. Start with the total income row.

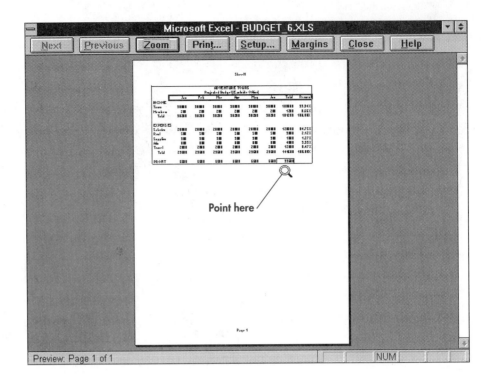

Point here

34. Select cells B7 through I7.

35. Choose C**e**lls from the Format menu.

36. Verify that the Border section is displayed.

37. Click on **T**op (indicating that the line will go on top of the selected cells).

38. Click on OK.

39. Preview the document.

40. Use the Zoom feature to view the changes.

41. Return to the worksheet.

Now complete the other total line.

42. On your own, insert the line on top of the total expenses row.

Next add a line above the profit row. The line will extend only to G17 because H17 already has a border.

43. Select cells B17 through G17.

44. On your own, display the Border options in the Format Cells dialog box.

Notice that there is a bottom line indicated for the selected cells. This is because row 17 is the bottom row of the worksheet, and the worksheet has a border around all of it. Now you need to specify a line above the selected row.

45. Click on **T**op.

46. Click on OK.

If you change your mind about a border, you can remove the border by clearing the Border options in the Format Cells dialog box. For example, if you want to remove the line on top of the profit row, you highlight the row and click on the Top option in the dialog box to deselect it. Do this now.

47. With the profit row highlighted (cells B17 through G17), choose Cells from the Format menu.

48. Click on the Top option in the Border section of the dialog box.

49. Click on OK.

50. Preview the document.

Continue by reinserting the top line for the profit row. But this time make it a double line.

51. Return to the worksheet.

52. On your own, insert a double line at the top of the profit row.

53. Preview the document.

54. View the changes and return to the worksheet.

WORKING WITH PATTERNS

Excel allows you to insert a **pattern** that gives a shading effect to parts of the worksheet. Figure 3.6 shows the column headings with a pattern. To insert a pattern, select the cell or cell range and display the Format Cells dialog box. Then choose the Patterns tab.

1. Select cells B3 through I3.

2. Choose Cells from the Format menu.

3.6

The column headings with a pattern

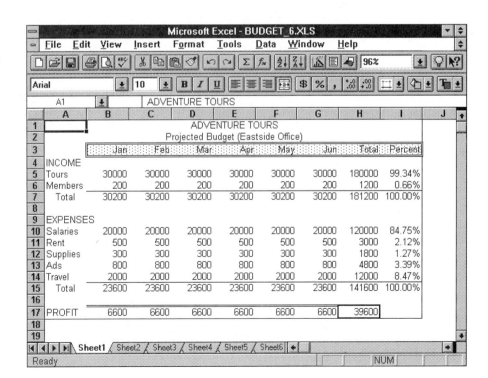

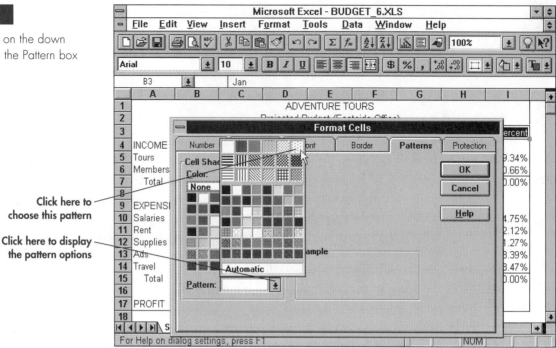

Click here to
choose this pattern

Click here to display
the pattern options

3. **Click on the Patterns tab.**

The Pattern option in the Cell Shading box is used to set the pattern.

4. **Click on the down arrow in the Pattern box to display the patterns (see Figure 3.7).**

5. **Click on the pattern with the fewest dots.**

6. **Notice that the Sample box displays the selected pattern.**

7. **Click on OK.**

The pattern is inserted in the selected cells.

8. **On your own, insert a pattern in cell H17, the overall profit.**

To remove a pattern, you choose the white square in the Pattern box.

9. **On your own, remove the pattern from cell H17.**

Before continuing, save the document.

10. **Save the document as bdgt_enh.**

FORMATTING NUMBERS

Excel allows you to change the way numbers are displayed. For example, you could display the same number (1000) with decimal places (1000.00), commas (1,000), or both (1,000.00). You could even display negative numbers with a minus sign and in red. The **number format** is up to you. However, you need

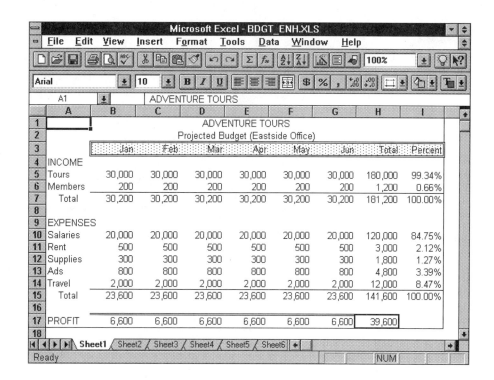

	A	B	C	D	E	F	G	H	I
1				ADVENTURE TOURS					
2				Projected Budget (Eastside Office)					
3		Jan	Feb	Mar	Apr	May	Jun	Total	Percent
4	INCOME								
5	Tours	30,000	30,000	30,000	30,000	30,000	30,000	180,000	99.34%
6	Members	200	200	200	200	200	200	1,200	0.66%
7	Total	30,200	30,200	30,200	30,200	30,200	30,200	181,200	100.00%
8									
9	EXPENSES								
10	Salaries	20,000	20,000	20,000	20,000	20,000	20,000	120,000	84.75%
11	Rent	500	500	500	500	500	500	3,000	2.12%
12	Supplies	300	300	300	300	300	300	1,800	1.27%
13	Ads	800	800	800	800	800	800	4,800	3.39%
14	Travel	2,000	2,000	2,000	2,000	2,000	2,000	12,000	8.47%
15	Total	23,600	23,600	23,600	23,600	23,600	23,600	141,600	100.00%
16									
17	PROFIT	6,600	6,600	6,600	6,600	6,600	6,600	39,600	
18									

to remember that the value of a number that you enter in a cell may be different from the number that appears in the worksheet. For instance, you might enter the number 555.75. If you format the cell to display no decimal places, the number will appear as 556 (rounding occurs for digits 5 and above). However, the value of the number remains 555.75, and this number is used in any calculations.

Figure 3.8 shows the budget with all the numbers formatted to display commas. In Chapter 1 you learned how to use the buttons on the Formatting toolbar to change the format of numbers. In this section you will use the Number section of the Format Cells dialog box. Start by formatting the numbers to display commas.

1. **Select cells B5 through H17.**

2. **Choose Cells from the Format menu.**

3. **Click on the Number tab.**

The Number section of the dialog box appears, showing several categories. Currently the All category is chosen and various number formats appear in the Format Codes list box. The 0 code displays no commas and no decimal places. The 0.00 code displays two decimal places and no commas. The #,##0.00 code displays commas and two decimal places. Select each of these codes and view the sample at the bottom of the dialog box. Figure 3.9 shows how the number (30000) in the active cell (B5) would display with the highlighted code.

4. **Click on 0.00.**

Notice that the sample changes to 30000.00 (see Figure 3.9).

5. **Click on #,##0.**

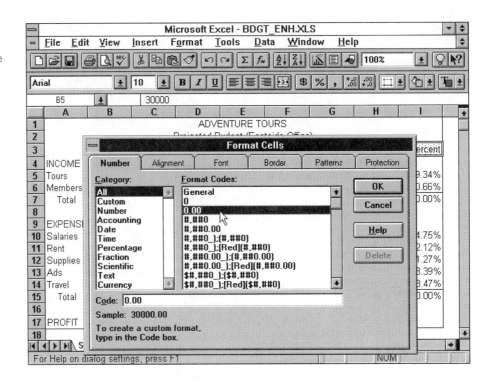

The sample changes to 30,000.

6. **Click on #,##0.00.**

The sample changes to 30,000.00. Now select the comma-only format and return to the workbook.

7. **Click on #,##0.**

8. **Click on OK.**

All the numbers now display commas. Continue by formatting the overall profit number in the **currency format** with no decimal places.

9. **Select H17.**

10. **Choose C̲ells from the Format menu.**

11. **Verify that the Number section is displayed.**

12. **Click on Currency in the Category list.**

Notice that the sample displays $39,600.

13. **Verify that the first format code is selected and click on OK.**

The overall profit number is displayed with a dollar sign and commas.

The Format Cells dialog box may be slower to work with than the Formatting toolbar, but there are more number-formatting options available.

CREATING TEXT BOXES AND ARROWS

Figure 3.10 shows a text box with text entered into it and an arrow added to the worksheet. A **text box** is useful for adding comments to a worksheet. This is because as you type a long entry, the words wrap around within the box. In addition, the text box is an object within the worksheet that can be moved, resized, and deleted. The arrow in Figure 3.10 is used to draw the reader's attention to a particular part of the worksheet. Both the text box and the arrow are created using buttons on the **Drawing toolbar** (see Figure 3.10). Start by displaying the Drawing toolbar. (*Note:* The Drawing toolbar may already be displayed on your screen; the following steps explain how to display the Drawing toolbar if it is not on the screen.)

1. **Click on View in the menu bar.**

2. **Click on Toolbars.**

The Toolbars dialog box appears.

3. **Click on Drawing to select (highlight) it (see Figure 3.11).**

4. **Click on OK.**

The Drawing toolbar appears beneath the Formatting toolbar. (*Note:* If the Drawing toolbar appears in another location, point to the toolbar, hold down the mouse button, and drag the toolbar to just beneath the Formatting toolbar.) Now create the text box. To do so, you select the Text Box button and move the pointer to the area in the worksheet where you want the box to appear. Then draw the box and type the text. You need to scroll the worksheet window to view row 28. This makes room for the text box you will create.

3.10

A text box and arrow added to the document

Drawing toolbar

Text Box button

Arrow button

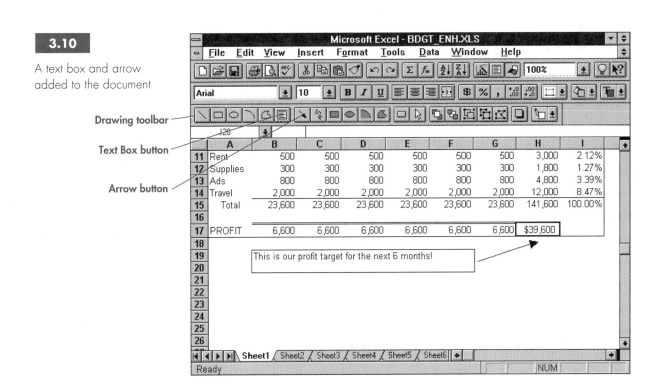

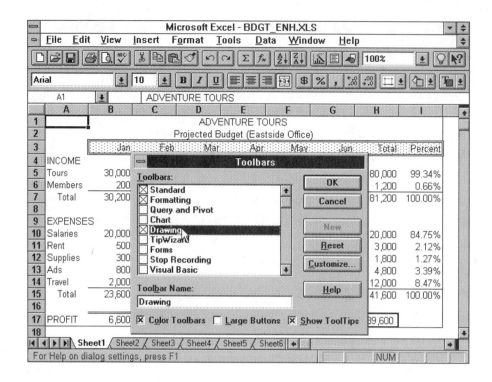

3.12

Pointing to the down
arrow in the vertical
scroll bar

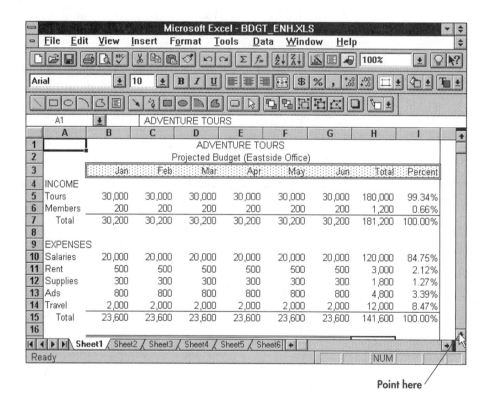

Point here

5. **Point to the down arrow in the vertical scroll bar (see Figure 3.12).**

6. **Click the mouse button until row 28 comes into view.**

7. **Click on the Text Box button (see Figure 3.10).**

8. **Point to cell B19.**

Notice that the pointer changes to a crosshair.

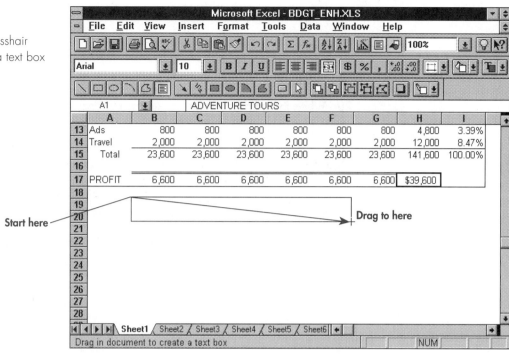

9. **Hold down the mouse button and drag the pointer diagonally to cell F20 (see Figure 3.13).**

10. **Release the mouse button.**

The box appears with a blinking vertical line that is used as a cursor. Any text you type will be inserted in the box starting at the cursor location.

11. **Type** This is our profit target for the next 6 months!

12. **Click on an area outside the text box to remove the cursor.**

The text box along with the text inside of it is considered an object that can be moved, resized, and deleted. To perform any of these operations, you must first select the text box by clicking on it.

13. **Point to the middle of the text box.**

14. **Click the mouse button.**

The border of the box changes to a broken line with eight handles. The handles are used to resize the box. The process is to point to a handle and, when the pointer changes to a double arrow, drag the handle away from the box to enlarge it or toward the box to reduce it. Figure 3.14 shows the box being enlarged by dragging the lower-right handle. Complete the following steps to duplicate Figure 3.14:

15. **Point to the lower-right handle of the box.**

16. **When the pointer changes to a double arrow, drag the handle diagonally down several rows.**

17. **Release the mouse button.**

Notice that the box is still selected. Now return the box to its original size.

18. On your own, return the box to its original size.

To move the box, you point to a border (not a handle) and drag the box to the new location. Figure 3.15 shows the box being moved down the worksheet.

19. Point to the bottom border (not a handle) of the box.

20. When the pointer changes to an arrow, drag the box down two rows.

3.14

Enlarging the text box by dragging the lower-right handle

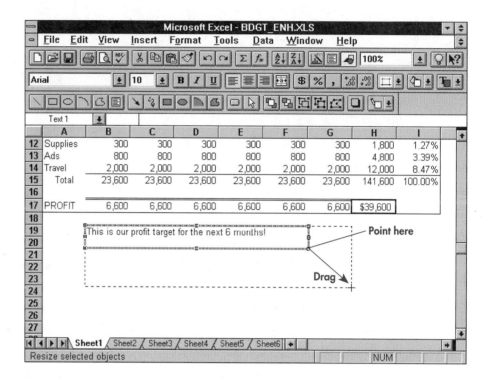

3.15

Moving the text box

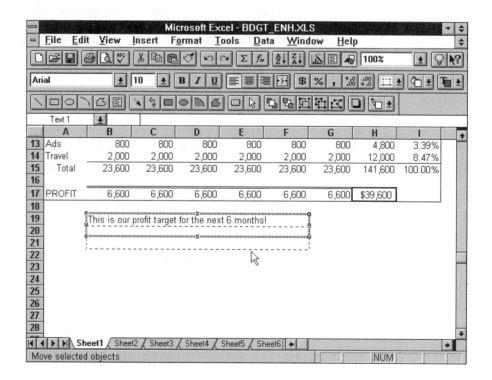

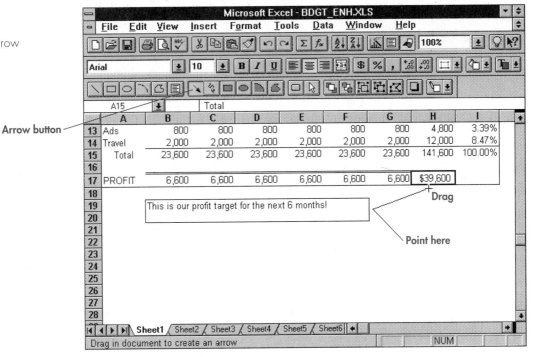

21. **Release the mouse button.**

22. **On your own, return the box to its original position.**

23. **Click on cell H17 to deselect the text box.**

To delete a box, you would select the box and press Delete. Now continue by inserting the arrow. The process is to click on the Arrow button on the Drawing toolbar and draw the arrow in the worksheet.

24. **Click on the Arrow button on the Drawing toolbar (see Figure 3.16).**

25. **Point to the right side of the text box (see Figure 3.16).**

26. **Hold down the mouse button and drag the pointer to just beneath cell H17.**

27. **Release the mouse button.**

The arrow appears with two handles, indicating that it is selected. Like the text box, the **arrow** is an object and can be resized, moved, and deleted. Now remove the Drawing toolbar from the screen.

28. **Choose Toolbars from the View menu.**

29. **Click on Drawing to deselect it.**

30. **Click on OK.**

CHANGING FONTS AND FONT SIZES

Figure 3.17 shows the heading *ADVENTURE TOURS* in a different font and font size. A **font** is a type design. Fonts can add variety to the appearance of a document and can even give it character. You can change the font using the Font options in the Format Cells dialog box. First select the heading.

1. **Select cell A1.**

2. **Choose Cells from the Format menu.**

3. **Click on the Font tab.**

The Font section of the Format Cells dialog box appears. You will use the dialog box to change the font to Times New Roman and the **font size** to 14. Figure 3.18 shows the completed dialog box. Start by scrolling the Font list to display Times New Roman.

4. **Point to the down arrow in the Font list scroll bar (see Figure 3.18).**

5. **Hold down the mouse button to scroll the list until Times New Roman appears. (*Note:* If Times New Roman is not available, choose another font.)**

6. **Click on Times New Roman to select it.**

7. **Change the font size to 14.**

Notice that the Preview box shows how the text will appear using the selected font and font size.

8. **Click on OK to leave the dialog box.**

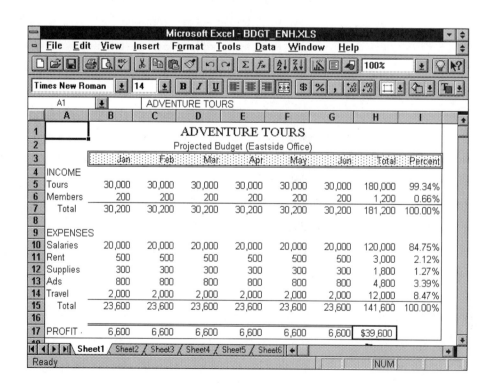

3.17

The heading
ADVENTURE TOURS
in a different font
and font size

EXCEL 5.0 FOR WINDOWS

3.18

The completed dialog box to change the font

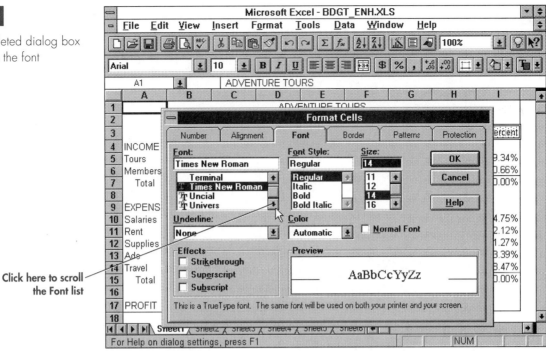

Click here to scroll the Font list

3.19

The heading *ADVENTURE TOURS* with the *A* and *T* formatted in a larger font

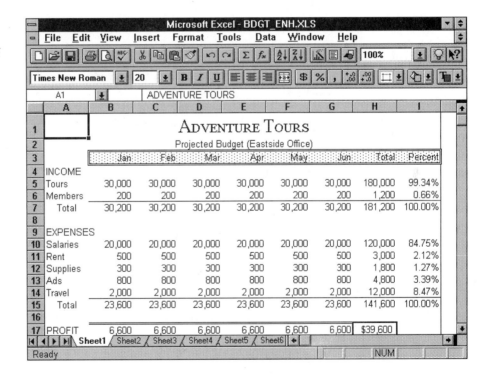

The heading is changed to the new font and font size.

Excel allows you to change the font and font size for individual characters in an entry. Figure 3.19 shows the *A* in *ADVENTURE* and the *T* in *TOURS* changed to size 20. The process is to select the cell with the entry and highlight the desired letter(s) in the formula bar. Then change the size (or font or style).

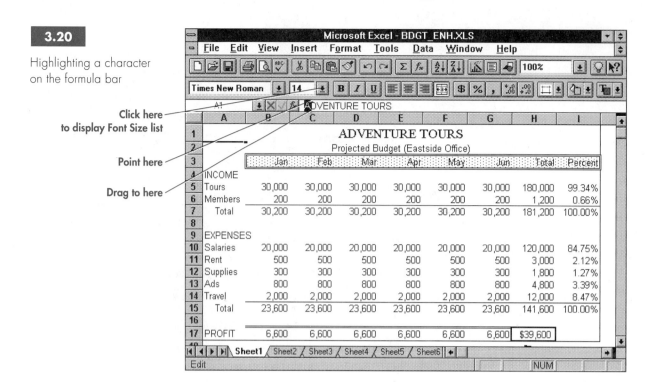

Click here
to display Font Size list

Point here

Drag to here

9. Verify that cell A1 is selected.

10. Point to before the *A* in *ADVENTURE* on the formula bar.

11. Drag the mouse pointer to highlight the *A* (see Figure 3.20).

Now use the Formatting toolbar to change the font size.

12. Click on the down arrow in the Font Size list box (see Figure 3.20).

13. Click on 20.

14. On your own, change the *T* in *TOURS* to size 20.

15. Click on the enter box on the formula bar.

CHANGING TYPE STYLES

Type styles, such as **bold** and *italic*, affect the way characters appear and are printed. They are useful for adding emphasis and drawing the reader's attention to a particular part of the document. Figure 3.21 shows the document with the following type style changes:

- The subheading *Projected Budget (Eastside Office)* is in italic type.

- The words *INCOME, EXPENSES,* and *PROFIT* are in bold type.

The Bold and Italic buttons on the Formatting toolbar are used to change type styles.

1. Click on cell A2 to select the subheading.

2. Click on the Italic button (see Figure 3.21).

Bold button

Italic button

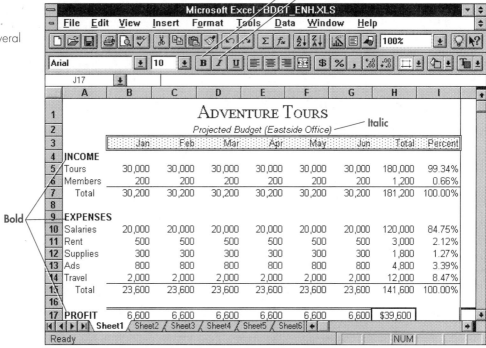

Italic

Bold

3. **Click on cell A4 to select** *INCOME*.

4. **Click on the Bold button (see Figure 3.21).**

5. **On your own, change** *EXPENSES* **and** *PROFIT* **to bold type.**

(*Note:* To turn off bold or italic, you select the cell with the text and click on the button again.)

This completes the section on changing type styles.

6. **Save the workbook as bdgt_dun.**

7. **Print the workbook and close it.**

USING AUTOFORMAT

The features you have been learning in this chapter allow you a great deal of flexibility in changing the appearance of a worksheet. If you are in a hurry to format a worksheet, you may want to take advantage of Excel's AutoFormat feature. With **AutoFormat** you can choose from a list of formats that can quickly enhance the appearance of a worksheet document. The process for using AutoFormat is to select the block of cells to apply the format to and then choose the AutoFormat command from the Format menu. A dialog box appears with a list of formats. You can choose a format and view an example before applying the format to your worksheet. You will use a workbook called budget_3, a three-month budget, to practice using the AutoFormat feature.

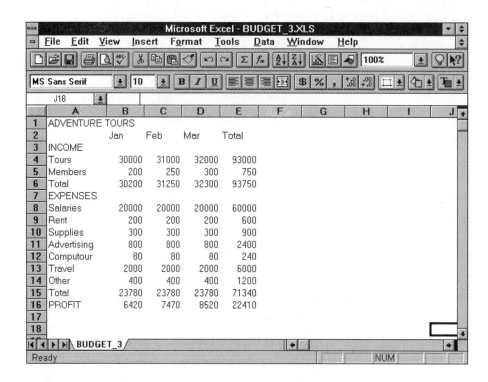

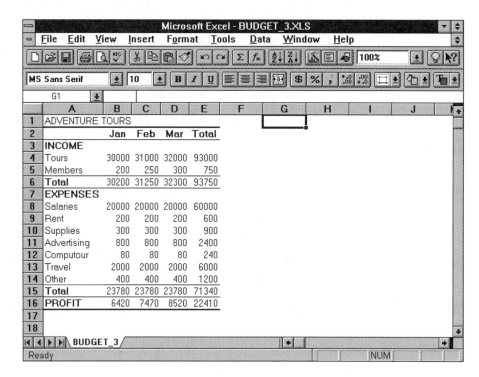

Figure 3.22 shows the worksheet without any formatting; that is, all of the default settings for font, font size, type style, and alignment were used. Figure 3.23 shows the same worksheet after applying an AutoFormat option.

1. **Open budget_3.**

2. **Select cells A2 through E16 (do not select row 1).**

3. **Choose _A_utoFormat from the Format menu.**

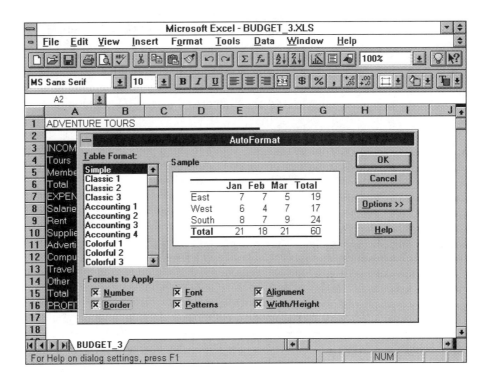

Figure 3.24 shows the AutoFormat dialog box that appears. A list of formats is displayed in the upper-left corner of the dialog box. An example of the highlighted format, Simple, is also displayed. In the bottom of the dialog box are the settings you can turn on and off. This allows you to tailor the format to your needs. (*Note:* If your dialog box does not display the settings, you can click on the Options button to display them.)

4. **If necessary, click on the Options button to display the settings.**

5. **Click on Border to turn it off.**

Notice the lines are removed from the sample.

6. **Click on Border to turn it on.**

Now apply this format to the worksheet.

7. **Click on OK.**

8. **Click on cell G1 to remove the highlight from the block.**

The worksheet appears with the formatting changes. It is important to understand that you can still make changes to the worksheet using the processes you have learned in this chapter. For example, if you wanted to add dollar signs, you could highlight the desired cells and change the numeric format. In addition, you can use the Undo command to undo this format and then select another.

9. **Choose Undo AutoFormat from the Edit menu.**

10. **If necessary, highlight cells A2 through E16.**

11. **Choose AutoFormat from the Format menu.**

Now take a moment to view the other formats.

12. Click on each format and view the sample.

13. When done viewing each format, click on the 3D Effects 1 format.

14. Click on OK.

15. Click on cell G1 to remove the highlight.

16. Save the workbook as Bdgt_fmt.

17. Print the worksheet.

18. Close the workbook.

CHAPTER REVIEW

KEY TERMS

align data	currency format	line
arrow	Drawing toolbar	number format
AutoFormat	font	pattern
bold	font size	text box
border	italic	type style
Center Across Columns button		

REVIEW QUESTIONS

1. Entries in a cell can be _____, _____, and _____ aligned.

2. **T F** Data that is center aligned across several cells displays in the middle of the selected cells but remains in the original cell.

3. Borders can be changed by choosing the _____ command in the _____ menu.

4. **T F** Choosing the Outline option in the Border section of the Format Cells dialog box places a border completely around the selected cells.

5. Specifying #,##0.00 as the format would display the entry 84711.164 as _____.

6. **T F** Text boxes and arrows are created using the commands from the Format menu.

7. **T F** Fonts can be used to add variety to the appearance of a document.

8. Examples of type styles are _____ and _____ type.

PROJECTS

1. Figure 3.25 shows a document that has been enhanced by:
   a. Increasing the column width for all columns (A–D) to 12
   b. Center-aligning the document heading across the document
   c. Changing the document heading to bold type
   d. Center-aligning the row headings
   e. Inserting single-line, double-line, and thick-line borders
   f. Inserting a pattern

3.25

The Income Forecast document with several enhancements

INCOME FORECAST BY OFFICE

	1995	1996	1997
Downtown	$450,000	500,000	540,000
Eastside	300,000	380,000	450,000
Total	750,000	880,000	990,000

The original worksheet is shown in Figure 1.1. If you completed Project 1 at the end of Chapter 1, you would have saved this workbook as ch1_p1. If so, you can open the workbook and make the changes. If not, you must first complete the original worksheet and then make the changes. Include your name at the bottom of the document. Save the workbook as ch3_p1, and then print the document.

2. Figure 3.26 shows a document that has been enhanced by:
   a. Inserting blank rows
   b. Adding a document heading, *SURVEY RESULTS*
   c. Changing the type style and enlarging the font for the document heading
   d. Changing the subheading (the question) to italic type
   e. Increasing the column widths for all columns (A–F) to 12
   f. Center-aligning the column headings
   g. Right-aligning the row headings
   h. Inserting single-line, double-line, and thick-line borders
   i. Inserting a pattern
   j. Displaying a text box with text and an arrow

SURVEY RESULTS

HOW LIKELY ARE YOU TO TAKE THE FOLLOWING TOURS WITHIN THE NEXT YEAR?

	Rafting	Trekking	Heli-ski	Safari	Mountain bike
Extremely	50	90	10	20	40
Very	75	65	15	25	60
Not very	25	35	20	35	80
Not at all	60	20	165	130	30
Total:	210	210	210	210	210

Let's do a special promotion for our trekking tours

The original worksheet is shown in Figure 1.1. If you completed Project 2 at the end of Chapter 1, you would have saved this workbook as ch1_p2. If so, you can open the workbook and make the changes. If not, you must first complete the original worksheet and then make the changes. Include your name at the bottom of the document. Save the workbook as ch3_p2, and then print the document. When done, hide the Drawing toolbar.

3. On your own, use the workbook associated with Project 4 in Chapter 2 and enhance the worksheet using the features you have learned in this chapter. Include your name at the bottom of the document. Save the workbook as ch3_p3, and then print the document without column headings and gridlines.

4. On your own, use the workbook associated with Project 3 in Chapter 1 and enhance the worksheet using the AutoFormat feature you have learned in this chapter. Include your name at the bottom of the document. Save the workbook as ch3_p4, and then print the document without column headings and gridlines.

5. On your own, use the workbook associated with Project 4 in Chapter 1 and enhance the worksheet using the AutoFormat feature you have learned in this chapter. Include your name at the bottom of the document. Save the workbook as ch3_p5, and then print the document without column headings and gridlines.

4

Working with Charts

IN THIS CHAPTER YOU WILL LEARN HOW TO:

- Define a chart

- Describe the relationship between worksheet data and a chart

- Use the ChartWizard to create a chart

- Change chart types

- Save a chart

- Print a chart

- Enhance charts

CHARTS AND WORKSHEETS

A **chart** is a drawing showing the relationships among numbers. The most common types of charts are column, line, and pie, as shown in Figures 4.1, 4.2, and 4.3, respectively. **Column charts** are useful in comparing two sets of data such as last year's income and this year's income. Figure 4.1 shows Adventure Tours's quarterly income for the previous and current years. The column chart makes it easy to compare the numbers quarter by quarter. **Line charts** are useful in analyzing trends. Figure 4.2 shows quarterly income for one year indicating a modest upward trend. **Pie charts** are useful in showing the relationship each part has to the whole. Figure 4.3 shows the part (percentage) each quarter is of the total yearly income.

4.1

A column chart

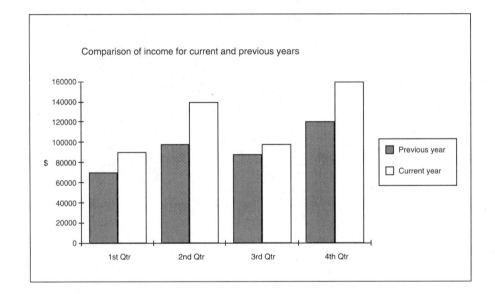

4.2

A line chart

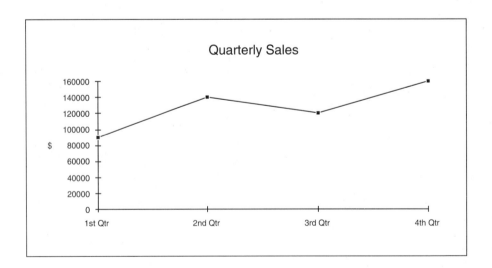

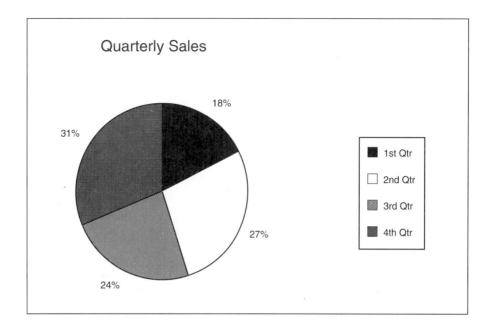

Usually, when you create a chart you need to specify two things: numbers and labels. Labels are such things as months or years. Thus, when you want to chart the income by month, the income is the numbers, and the months (Jan, Feb, Mar, . . .) are the labels. Normally, for column and line charts the numbers are plotted vertically on the **y axis**, and the labels are plotted horizontally on the **x axis** (see Figure 4.4, which shows a chart of sales by month). A pie chart does not use axes but rather adds the numbers together and uses the part that each label is of the total to create the chart. Thus, if January income was one-third of the total income for the four-month period, its slice would be one-third of the pie.

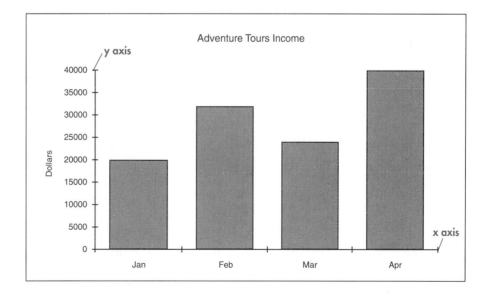

(*Note:* If you are using a color monitor, the charts you create will be displayed in color. However, in this book we will represent the colors in various shades of gray.)

CREATING A CHART

To create a chart, you develop a new, or open an existing, workbook; select the cells that contain the data to be used in the chart; and use the ChartWizard tool to create the chart. Because worksheets comprise numbers, they can easily be used as a basis for creating charts. Figure 4.5 shows a worksheet with Adventure Tours's income for a four-month period. You will develop this worksheet and use the data to create a series of charts.

1. **Start Excel.**

2. **On your own, create the worksheet shown in Figure 4.5.**

3. **Right-align the month headings.**

4. **Save the workbook as inc_4mo.**

Excel provides **ChartWizard**, a tool that helps you develop charts. ChartWizard displays a series of dialog boxes that allow you to specify the data to be used in the chart, the type of chart, and the chart titles. The ChartWizard button is found on the Standard toolbar (see Figure 4.5). Before choosing the ChartWizard tool, you must select the cell range that contains the data to be included in the chart. In this case the data will be the month headings and the income numbers.

4.5

The worksheet used to create a chart

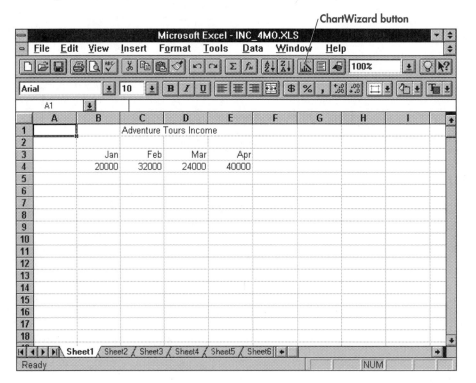

EXCEL 5.0 FOR WINDOWS

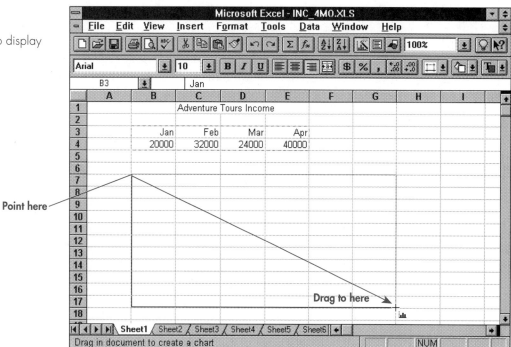

5. **Select cells B3 through E4.**

6. **Click on the ChartWizard button.**

7. **Point to cell B7.**

Notice that the pointer changes to a crosshair and the ChartWizard icon, and the message on the status line at the bottom of the window says: Drag in document to create a chart. You need to use the crosshair to draw a box that will become the area for the chart. Figure 4.6 shows the process.

8. **Hold down the mouse button and drag the pointer diagonally to cell G17.**

9. **Release the mouse button.**

ChartWizard's first dialog box, Step 1 of 5, is displayed. This dialog box is used to confirm that the cell range you have selected is correct. If not, the dialog box allows you to make a change. The range should be =$B$3:$E$4.

10. **Click on the Next button in the Step 1 dialog box to continue.**

Step 2 allows you to choose a chart type. The Column chart is highlighted, meaning it is currently selected. If you wanted a different chart type, you would click on it. Leave the chart type as Column.

11. **Click on the Next button in the Step 2 dialog box.**

Step 3 shows ten different variations of the Column chart. Select number 1.

12. **Click on chart 1.**

13. **Click on the Next button in the Step 3 dialog box.**

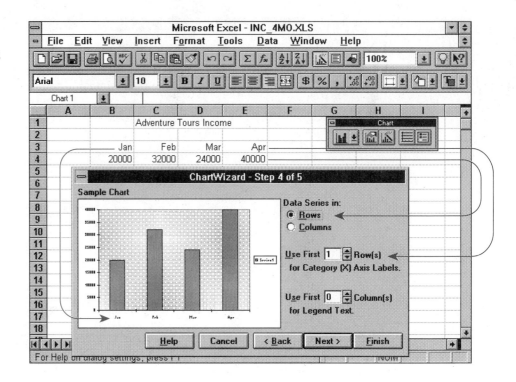

Step 4 displays the chart as you have defined it so far. Refer to Figure 4.7 as you read the following explanation of the options in this dialog box:

- Data Series in. The Rows option is selected, indicating that the data (labels and numbers) to be charted is in rows, not columns.

- Use First <u>1</u> Row(s) for Category (X) Axis Labels. This indicates that the first row in the range (row 3) contains the labels (Jan, Feb, Mar, Apr) that appear on the x axis.

- Use First <u>0</u> Column(s) for Legend Text. This indicates that no data will be used for a legend. A legend is not needed on this chart because there is only one series of numbers (income).

These options are correct.

14. Click on the Next button in the Step 4 dialog box.

Step 5 appears, allowing you to add a chart legend and chart titles. No legend is necessary because there is only one data series (income). However, there is no indication of what the chart represents and what the numbers represent. Thus, you will add a chart title and a y-axis title. Figure 4.8 shows the completed dialog box.

15. Click on <u>N</u>o under the Add a Legend? option.

16. Point inside the <u>C</u>hart Title box.

17. Click the mouse button to display a cursor.

18. Type Adventure Tours Income

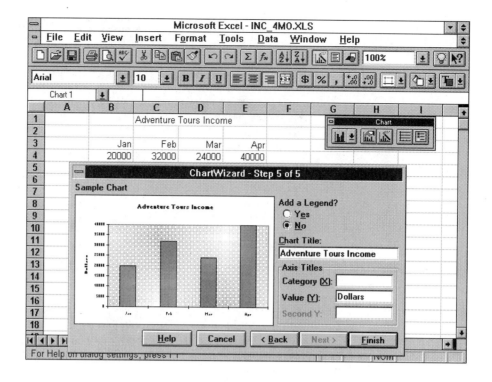

19. **Click inside the Value (Y) box.**

20. **Type** Dollars

The changes you make are displayed in the Sample Chart box.

21. **Click on the Finish button to complete the chart.**

The chart is displayed in the area you specified, B7 through G17. At this point there are two parts to the worksheet: the data and the chart. Although they are linked, you work with them separately. The chart is considered an object within the worksheet, and to work with the chart, it must be selected. Notice that there are handles surrounding the chart, indicating that it is selected. To deselect the chart (so you can work with the worksheet data), you click outside the chart.

22. **Click on an area outside the chart.**

The handles are removed from the chart. To select the chart, click on it once.

23. **Click on the chart.**

The handles reappear.

RESIZING, MOVING, AND DELETING CHARTS

Because the chart is an object, it can be resized, moved, and deleted. In Chapter 3 you worked with text boxes. The process is the same: To resize the chart, drag a handle; to move a chart, drag a border; to delete a chart, press

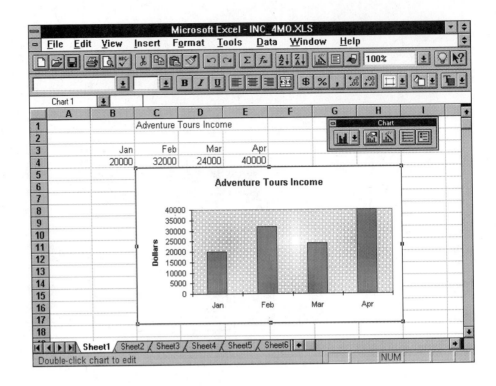

Delete. Take a moment to practice resizing and moving the chart. Figure 4.9 shows the chart enlarged and moved to the right. Complete the following steps to duplicate this figure:

1. Point to the top middle handle and drag the border up two rows.

2. Point to a border (not to a handle) and drag the chart to the right one column.

3. On your own, return the chart to its original position (but leave the chart size enlarged).

EDITING THE NUMBERS IN A CHART

You can change the numbers in the worksheet, and the chart will automatically be adjusted. Practice this by changing the January income to 60000.

1. Click on cell B4.

2. Type 60000

3. Click on the enter box on the formula bar.

Notice that the chart is adjusted to reflect the new number.

4. On your own, change the income for January back to 20000.

SAVING A CHART

After developing a chart, you can save the workbook, and the chart will be saved with it. Later, when you open the workbook, the chart will be opened also.

1. Save the workbook as inc_4moc.

PRINTING A CHART

A chart can be printed with or without the worksheet. If you print a chart with the worksheet, it will print in the size you have drawn it. Use the Print Preview command to see how the worksheet and chart will print.

1. Click on the Print Preview button.
2. After viewing the document, click on Print.
3. Click on OK in the Print dialog box.

If you want to print the chart separately, you must activate it before giving the Print command.

ACTIVATING A CHART

Even though the chart is part of the worksheet, you can activate it and make changes, save it, and print it separately from the worksheet. When you select a chart, the message on the status line near the bottom of the window says: Double-click chart to edit.

1. Click on the chart to select it and then read the status line.
2. Double-click the mouse button.

The chart is activated as indicated by a slanted-line border.

CHANGING CHART TYPES

Excel provides dozens of chart types. In this section you will display several types using the AutoFormat command in the Format menu.

1. Click on Format in the menu bar.
2. Click on AutoFormat.

A list of chart types is displayed in the Galleries list box. Column is highlighted, indicating that it is the type being used. Each of these types has several variations. Ten different formats of column charts are displayed. Some of these are used when you have more than one **data series**. For example, a chart of income for the current year and income for the previous year would have two data series. The chart 1 format would display these two data series side-by-side. Other charts display gridlines (chart 6) or the actual numbers as part of the chart (chart 7). Take a moment to display these formats.

3. Click on Format 6.

4. Click on OK.

The chart is displayed with gridlines.

5. Choose AutoFormat from the Format menu.

6. Click on Format 7.

7. Click on OK.

The numbers are displayed above the columns. Now choose another chart type.

8. Choose AutoFormat from the Format menu.

9. Click on Line in the Galleries list box.

Ten formats for line charts appear. The first three types are typical charts that show variations in the use of lines and markers. **Markers** are the small rectangular boxes that appear at each data point (that is, 20000, 32000, 24000, and 40000). Format 1 is currently selected.

10. Click on OK to display the line chart.

Take a moment to study the chart. Notice that the markers appear at each data point. Format 2 removes the markers from the chart. Choose this chart format.

11. Choose AutoFormat from the Format menu.

This time use the shortcut for choosing a chart type: double-click on it.

12. Double-click on Line Format 2.

Notice that the markers are removed from the chart.

13. On your own, display Line Format 3, which shows only the markers.

14. On your own, display Line Format 4, which shows lines, markers, and gridlines.

Now display some of the pie charts.

15. Display the AutoFormat dialog box.

16. Choose Pie from the Galleries list.

17. Double-click on Pie Format 1.

The pie chart is displayed with a title but no labels.

18. On your own, change the chart to Pie Format 7.

This chart shows the labels and the percent that each slice is of the whole pie.

19. **On your own, change the chart to Pie Format 5.**

Only the labels appear. In addition to using the AutoFormat command, you can use Excel's Chart toolbar to change the chart type.

USING THE CHART TOOLBAR

The **Chart toolbar** can be displayed using the Toolbars command in the View menu. (*Note:* Your computer may automatically display the Chart toolbar when the chart is activated.) The Chart toolbar provides shortcuts to formatting a chart. One of the buttons, Chart Type, allows you to quickly change the type of chart. Not all types are available from the Chart toolbar. Figure 4.10 identifies the Chart Type button on the Chart toolbar. First, if necessary, display the Chart toolbar.

1. **Choose Toolbars from the View menu.**

2. **Click on Chart in the Toolbars list.**

3. **Click on OK.**

(*Note:* The Chart toolbar may appear as a "floating" bar onscreen, as shown in Figure 4.10, or it may appear across the top, bottom, or right side of the worksheet.)

4.10

Changing the chart type using the Chart toolbar

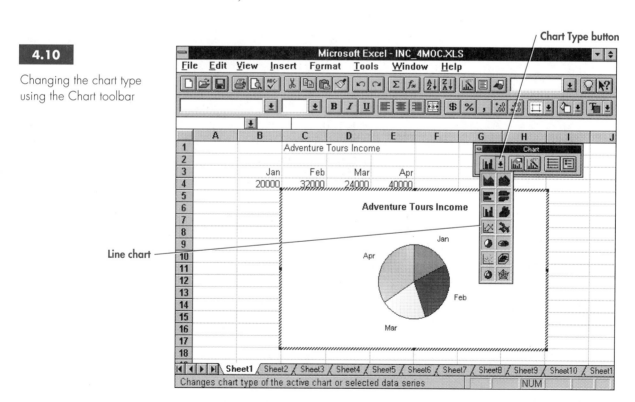

Chart Type button

Line chart

4. Click on the down arrow next to the Chart Type button on the Chart toolbar (see Figure 4.10).

5. Click on the line-type option in the list that appears (see Figure 4.10).

6. On your own, use the Chart toolbar to change the chart type to column.

PRINTING THE CHART SEPARATE FROM THE WORKSHEET

The chart can be printed apart from the worksheet when the chart is activated. Use the Print Preview command to see how the chart will print on the page.

1. Click on the Print Preview button on the Standard toolbar.

Notice that the chart is positioned in the middle of the page with the chart name at the top of the page (in the header) and the page number at the bottom of the page (in the footer). It is also displayed on the page sideways, in landscape orientation. You can change the page orientation by using the Setup button and choosing Portrait.

2. Click on the Setup button.

3. If necessary, select the Page tab in the dialog box.

4. Click on Portrait in the Orientation box.

5. Click on OK.

You can adjust the size of the chart and the position on the page by changing the margins.

6. Click on the Margins button near the top of the window.

The margins, represented by dotted lines, are displayed on the page. You can adjust the margins by dragging the lines. Figure 4.11 shows the margins after dragging the bottom line up and the left line to the right. Complete the following steps to duplicate this figure:

7. Point to the bottom margin line (see Figure 4.12).

8. When the pointer changes to a double arrow, hold down the mouse button and drag the line up to the middle of the page.

9. Release the mouse button.

10. On your own, drag the left margin line to the middle of the page.

Your screen should resemble Figure 4.11. Now print the chart.

11. Click on the Margins button to remove the margin lines.

12. Click on the Print button.

13. Click on OK.

4.11

The margin lines after dragging the bottom line up and the left line to the right

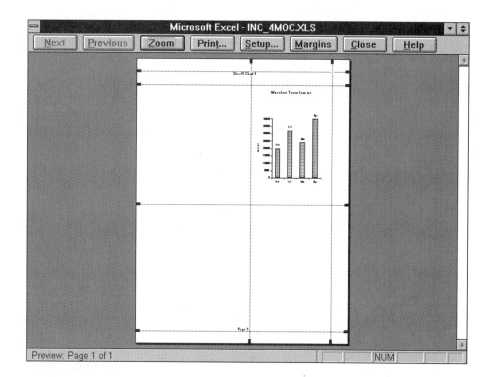

4.12

Pointing to the bottom margin line

Point here

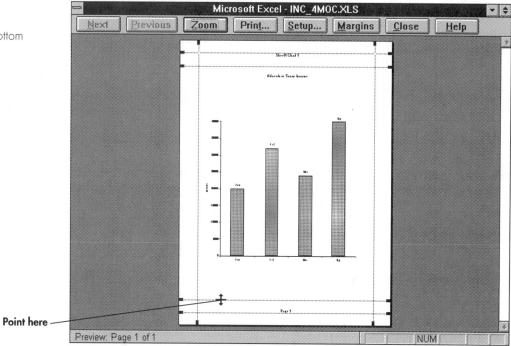

Until now you have been working with a single data series (income for January through April). Figure 4.13 shows a chart with a second data series (expenses for January through April) added to the worksheet and plotted on the chart. There are two ways to develop this chart. You could start with an existing chart and copy the new data series to it. To do so, you select the new numbers, choose Copy from the Edit menu, activate the chart, and choose Paste from the Edit menu. Another method for creating the chart is to develop an entirely new chart. You will create a new chart using the ChartWizard. This time you need to add and select the words *Income* and *Expenses*. These are used for a legend to help distinguish between the two data series. Start by deleting the current chart.

1. **Verify that the chart is selected.**

(*Note:* The handles will appear, but not the slanted-line border. If the slanted-line border appears, click once in the worksheet to remove the slanted-line border and keep the handles.)

2. **Press** Delete.

The chart disappears. Next enter the new data.

3. **Select cell A4.**

4. **Type** Income

5. **Select cell A5.**

6. **Type** Expenses

4.13

A chart with two
data series

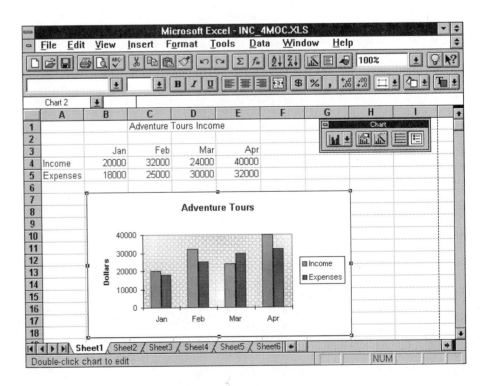

7. **Select cell B5.**

8. **Type** 18000

9. **On your own, enter the other numbers (see Figure 4.13).**

10. **Select cells A3 through E5.**

11. **Click on the ChartWizard tool.**

12. **Draw a box that will be used to display the chart.**

13. **On your own, work through steps 1, 2, and 3 to create a column chart without gridlines. Stop at step 4.**

Figure 4.14 shows step 4. Notice that the Use First _ Column(s) for Legend Text option displays 1. This means that the text (Income, Expenses) in the first column of the cell range (column A) is used for a legend. Notice the legend displayed in the Sample Chart box. The legend tells which numbers are income and which are expenses.

14. **Click on Next to move to step 5.**

Figure 4.15 shows the completed dialog box to enter a chart title and a y-axis title.

15. **Duplicate Figure 4.15.**

16. **Click on the Finish button to complete the chart.**

17. **Save the workbook as inc_exp.**

18. **Double-click on the chart to activate it.**

The column chart makes it easy to compare income and expenses month by month. Take a moment to view other chart types using the AutoFormat dialog box.

4.14

Step 4 of the ChartWizard showing that the first column is used for the legend

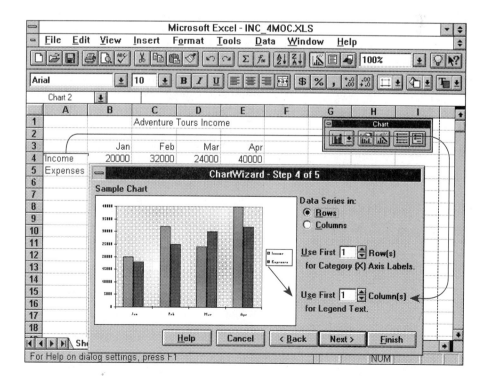

4.15

The completed dialog box to enter chart titles

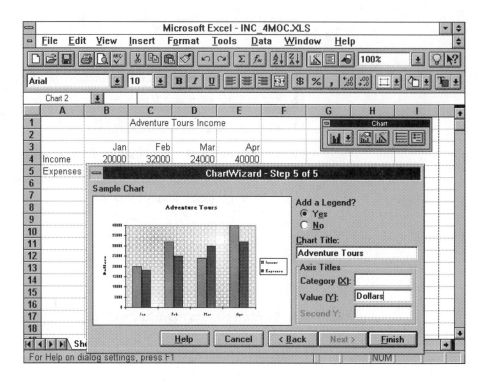

19. **Display the AutoFormat dialog box.**

20. **Select Line from the Galleries list.**

21. **Double-click on Format 1.**

The line chart shows expenses moving up in a fairly gradual manner. But income fluctuates sharply, including a steep decline in March to below expenses.

22. **Display the AutoFormat dialog box.**

23. **Choose Combination from the Galleries list.**

24. **Double-click on Format 1.**

This **combination chart** combines a column and a line.

25. **On your own, change the chart type to a 3-D column.**

This chart displays as a three-dimensional object.

26. **On your own, change the chart type to Column and the format to 1.**

CHANGING THE APPEARANCE OF A CHART

Excel provides several ways in which you can enhance the appearance of a chart and draw the reader's attention to a part of the chart. Figure 4.16 shows the chart with the following changes:

- New words are added to the chart title, the words are italicized, and they are in a larger font.

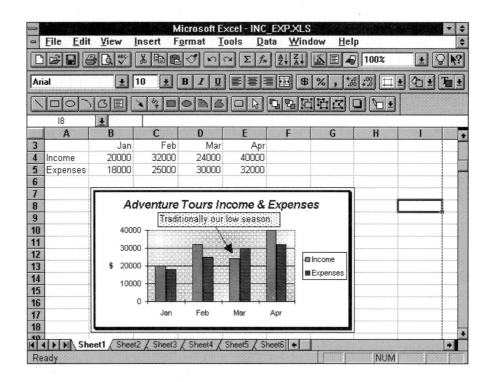

- The y-axis title is changed to a dollar sign ($).

- Gridlines are added to the chart.

- A text box with a border and pattern is added to the chart.

- An arrow is added to the chart.

- A border with a shadow is placed around the chart.

You will duplicate Figure 4.16.

A chart is made up of several objects: titles, legends, columns, text boxes, arrows, and so on. All these objects can be changed; for example, the chart title can be changed by adding words and increasing the font size. Before you make any changes to an object, you must activate the chart and select the object by clicking on it. Now make changes to the title.

1. **With the chart activated, click on the title.**

Handles appear, indicating that the title is selected. The first change is to add the words *Income & Expenses*.

2. **Place the mouse pointer after the *s* in *Tours* and click the mouse button to display the cursor.**

3. **Press the spacebar once.**

4. **Type** Income & Expenses

Next you will increase the font size for the title. This can be done by highlighting the title and using the Selected Chart Title command from the Format menu or using the Font Size list on the Formatting toolbar.

5. **Drag the mouse across the title to highlight it.**

6. **Choose 12 from the Font Size list.**

Next change the title to italic type.

7. **Click on the Italic button on the Formatting toolbar.**

Now change the y-axis title from *Dollars* to *$*.

8. **Click on *Dollars* to select it.**

9. **Type $**

10. **Press** ⌨Enter.

Notice that the $ is turned horizontally. You can use the Alignment section of the Format Axis Title dialog box to turn it vertically.

11. **Choose Selected Axis Title from the Format menu.**

12. **Click on the Alignment tab.**

The Orientation box indicates how the selected text is aligned. Select the orientation shown in Figure 4.17.

13. **Click on the orientation shown in Figure 4.17.**

14. **Click on OK.**

The $ is displayed vertically. Next add gridlines to the chart.

15. **Click on the Horizontal Gridlines button on the Chart toolbar (see Figure 4.18).**

Now add a text box with the words *Traditionally our low season*. Then format the text box with a border and a pattern. First display the Drawing toolbar.

16. **Choose Toolbars from the View menu.**

4.17

Changing the orientation of the selected text

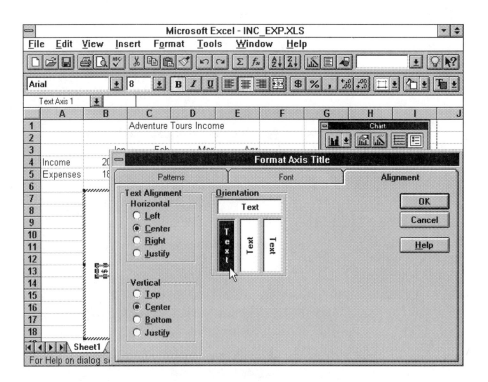

4.18

Adding horizontal gridlines to the chart using the Chart toolbar

Horizontal Gridlines button

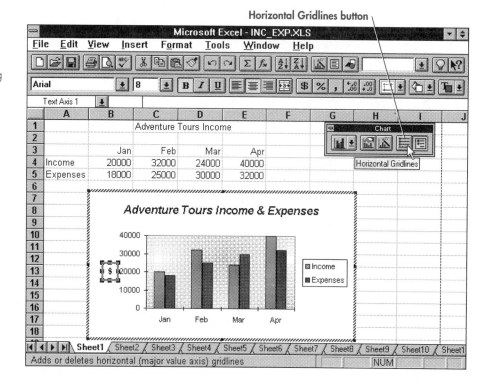

17. **Click on Drawing.**

18. **Click on OK.**

Now you need to draw the box that will contain the text.

19. **Click on the Text Box button (see Figure 4.19).**

20. **Point to below the *A* in *Adventure*.**

4.19

Using the Text Box button to add text to the chart

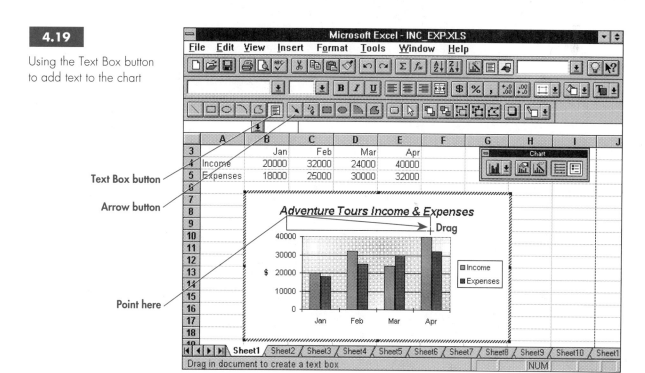

21. Hold down the mouse button and drag the mouse pointer to draw the text box (see Figure 4.19).

22. **Release** the mouse button.

23. **Type** Traditionally our low season.

The insertion point is still visible. To remove the insertion point, you need to point away from the text box and click the mouse button.

24. **Point** to above the legend.

25. **Click** the mouse button.

You can resize and reposition the text box as follows.

26. **Double-click** on the word *Traditionally* to select the text box.

27. **Point** to the handle on the right of the text box (see Figure 4.20).

28. **Hold** down the mouse button.

29. **When** the pointer changes to a double arrow, drag the pointer to the left (but not too close to the word *season*).

30. **Release** the mouse button.

31. **Point** to a border (not a handle) of the text box.

32. **Hold** down the mouse button and drag the border to center the text box across the chart.

Next format the text box by placing a border around it and a pattern within it. You can format the text box using the Selected Object command from the Format menu.

4.20

Resizing the text box

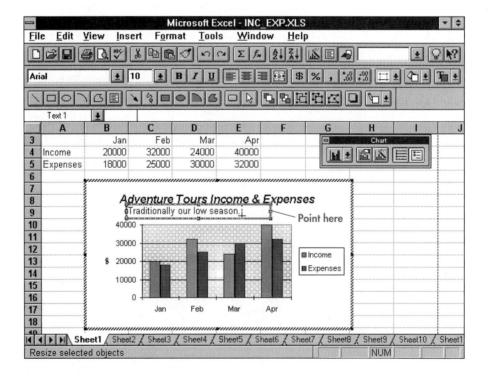

33. With the text box still selected, click on Format in the menu bar.

34. Click on Selected Object.

35. If necessary, click on the Patterns tab.

The Patterns section of the Format Object dialog box allows you to specify a pattern and a border.

36. Click on Custom in the Border box.

This will create a single-line border around the text box. You need to specify the type of pattern.

37. Click on the down arrow next to the Pattern box.

This displays a list of patterns.

38. Click on the pattern with the fewest dots.

39. Click on OK.

The text box displays a border and pattern. Now add an arrow.

40. Click on the Arrow button on the Drawing toolbar (see Figure 4.19).

41. Point to below the text box, under the word *our*.

42. Hold down the mouse button and drag the pointer to just above the March income column.

43. Release the mouse button.

The final change you will make to the chart is to add a border with a shadow around the entire chart.

44. Click above the legend to select the chart. The handles surrounding the entire chart should be displayed.

45. Choose Selected Chart Area from the Format menu.

46. If necessary, click on the Patterns tab to display this section of the dialog box.

47. Click on Shadow in the Border box.

48. Click on Custom in the Border box.

Now change the weight of the border to produce a thicker line.

49. Click on the down arrow in the Weight box (see Figure 4.21).

50. Point to the thickest line (see Figure 4.21).

51. Click the mouse button to select the line.

52. Click on OK to return to the chart.

53. Double-click outside the chart to deselect it.

Your screen should resemble Figure 4.16. Now print the worksheet and chart.

54. Choose Print from the File menu.

55. Click on OK.

4.21

Changing the weight of the line bordering the chart

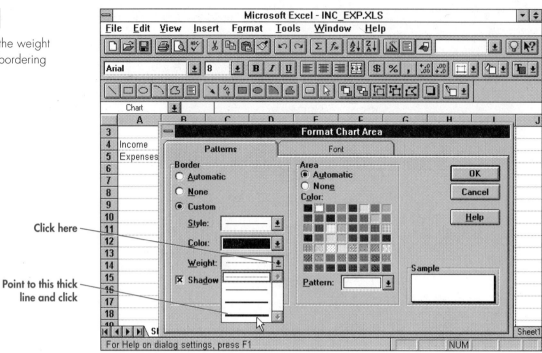

This completes the section on making changes to the chart. Now save the document.

56. Save the workbook as inc_exp2.

57. Close the workbook.

CHAPTER REVIEW

KEY TERMS

chart	combination chart	pie chart
Chart toolbar	data series	x axis
ChartWizard	line chart	y axis
column chart	markers	

REVIEW QUESTIONS

1. A chart is a drawing showing the relationships among _____.

2. The most common types of charts are _____, _____, and _____.

3. Normally, the numbers are plotted vertically on the _____ axis of a chart.

4. To create a chart, you use the _____ tool.

5. **T F** A chart is considered an object and can be resized, moved, and deleted.

6. To activate a chart, you _____ click on the chart.

7. The _____ button on the Chart toolbar is used to change chart types.

8. **T F** Charts cannot be saved separate from the workbook used to create them.

PROJECTS

1. Develop the line chart shown in Figure 4.2. The numbers for the quarters are 1st Qtr, 90000; 2nd Qtr, 140000; 3rd Qtr, 120000; 4th Qtr, 160000. Include your name on the worksheet. Save the workbook as ch4_p1. Print the worksheet and the chart as one document.

2. Using the workbook for Project 1, develop the pie chart shown in Figure 4.3. Save the workbook as ch4_p2, and then print the chart only.

3. Develop a worksheet with the following data. Using the worksheet, create the column chart shown in Figure 4.1. Save the workbook as ch4_p3, and then print the chart.

	1st Qtr	2nd Qtr	3rd Qtr	4th Qtr
Previous year	70000	98000	88000	120000
Current year	90000	140000	98000	160000

4. Enhance the chart created in Project 3 so that it duplicates Figure 4.22. Save the workbook as ch4_p4, and then print the chart.

4.22

A chart with several enhancements

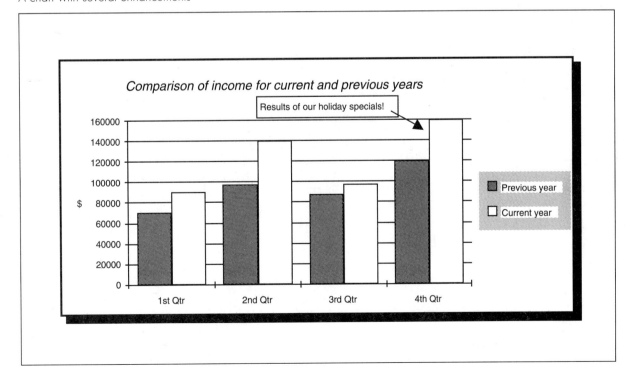

5

Working with Large Worksheets

Until now you have been working primarily with relatively small worksheets, that is, those that will fit on the screen and on a single sheet of paper. When you work with large worksheets, you need to know how to change the view so that more of the worksheet appears onscreen. You also need to know how to manipulate the worksheet to print more of the worksheet on one page of paper.

VIEWING DIFFERENT PARTS OF A WORKSHEET

Figure 5.1 shows the screen view of a large worksheet, budget12. This document is a twelve-month budget for Adventure Tours. Notice that only columns A through I and rows 1 through 18 are in view. You can use the Full Screen command to view more rows of a worksheet. The **Full Screen command** removes the title bar, the toolbars, and the status bar.

1. **Start Excel.**

2. **Open budget12.xls.**

3. **Choose Full Screen from the View menu.**

Several more rows are displayed, including the profit row. Notice that the Full Screen button appears on the worksheet. If you click on this button, the various bars will reappear.

4. **Click on the Full Screen button to return to the original view.**

Whereas the Full Screen command allows you to view more rows, the **Zoom command** can be used to view more columns as well as more rows. The Zoom

5.1

The screen view of a large worksheet

	A	B	C	D	E	F	G	H	I	J	K	L	M	N	O
1							ADVENTURE TOURS								
2							Proposed Budget (Eastside Office)								
3		Jan	Feb	Mar	Apr	May	Jun	Jul	Aug	Sep	Oct	Nov	Dec	Total	Percent
4															
5	INCOME														
6	Tours	30,000	31,000	32,000	33,000	34,000	35,000	36,000	37,000	38,000	39,000	40,000	41,000	426,000	98.7%
7	Members	200	250	300	350	400	450	500	550	600	650	700	750	5,700	1.3%
8	Total	30,200	31,250	32,300	33,350	34,400	35,450	36,500	37,550	38,600	39,650	40,700	41,750	431,700	100.0%
9															
10	EXPENSES														
11	Salaries	20,000	20,000	20,000	20,000	20,000	21,000	22,050	23,153	24,310	25,526	26,802	28,142	270,982	84.1%
12	Rent	200	200	200	200	200	200	200	200	200	200	200	200	2,400	0.7%
13	Utilities	500	500	500	500	500	500	500	500	500	500	500	500	6,000	1.9%
14	Supplies	300	300	300	300	300	300	300	300	300	300	300	300	3,600	1.1%
15	Advertising	800	800	800	800	800	800	800	800	800	800	800	800	9,600	3.0%
16	Computour	80	80	80	80	80	80	80	80	80	80	80	80	960	0.3%
17	Travel	2,000	2,000	2,000	2,000	2,000	2,000	2,000	2,000	2,000	2,000	2,000	2,000	24,000	7.4%
18	Other	400	400	400	400	400	400	400	400	400	400	400	400	4,800	1.5%
19	Total	24,280	24,280	24,280	24,280	24,280	25,280	26,330	27,433	28,590	29,806	31,082	32,422	322,342	100.0%
20															
21	PROFIT	5,920	6,970	8,020	9,070	10,120	10,170	10,170	10,118	10,010	9,844	9,618	9,328	109,358	

Screen

EXCEL 5.0 FOR WINDOWS

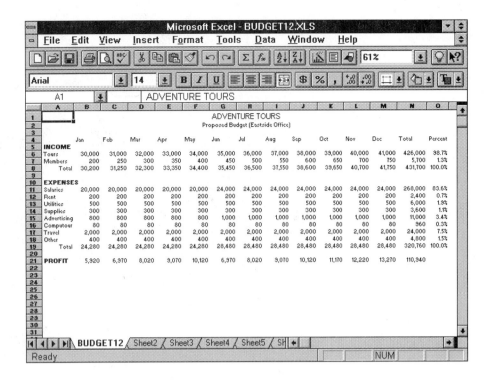

command from the View menu (or the Zoom Control tool on the Standard toolbar) allows you to reduce the size of the entries so more of the worksheet fits onscreen. Using this command, you can specify how much to reduce the size of the entries. Figure 5.2 shows the entries reduced so the entire worksheet is in view.

5. Choose Zoom from the View menu.

The Zoom dialog box appears, allowing you to select from several different magnifications. The 100% option is the current view and can be selected if you want to return to this view. The 200% option doubles the size of the worksheet, the 75% option reduces the worksheet to three-quarters of its original size, and so forth. The Custom option allows you to specify any percentage.

6. Click on 75%.

7. Click on OK.

Almost the entire worksheet is displayed using this view.

8. Choose Zoom from the View menu.

9. Double-click on 50%.

All the worksheet data is displayed. However, the numbers are somewhat difficult to read. The blank columns at the right of the worksheet indicate that there is room to increase the worksheet size and still fit it on the screen. The **Fit Selection option** from the Zoom dialog box uses the whole screen to display the worksheet data. A shortcut is to use the Zoom Control tool. Start by selecting all the data.

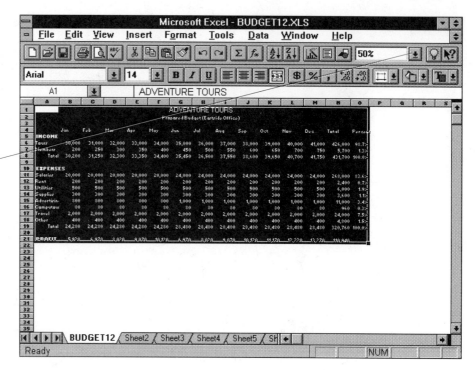

Click here to display the
Zoom options

10. **Select cells A1 through O21 (see Figure 5.3).**

11. **Click on the down arrow next to the Zoom Control tool (see Figure 5.3).**

12. **Click on Selection.**

Again, all the data is displayed. This time the entire width of the screen is used. Notice the percent displayed in the Zoom Control box on the toolbar. Remember, you have changed how you are viewing the worksheet, not how it will print. It will print in the size shown in the 100% view. Now return the view to 100%.

13. **On your own, use the Zoom dialog box or the Zoom Control tool to return the view to 100%.**

Changing the magnification is a way to view different parts of a large worksheet. However, as you reduce the magnification, the size of the entries are reduced, and the document becomes harder to read. Another way to view different parts of a document is to split the worksheet.

SPLITTING A WORKSHEET

Assume you want to see the effect on total expenses of increasing the travel expense in March to $4,500. The total expenses are located in column N, and the March expenses are in column D. Using the 100% view (with the standard character size and column width), you cannot view both of these columns at one time. However, by splitting the worksheet you can view two different parts of the worksheet at the same time. Figure 5.4 shows the worksheet after splitting it at column E. Notice that columns A through D are displayed at the

5.4

The worksheet after splitting it at column E

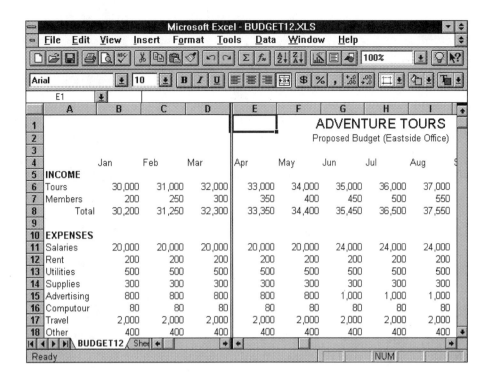

5.5

The right side scrolled to display columns N and O

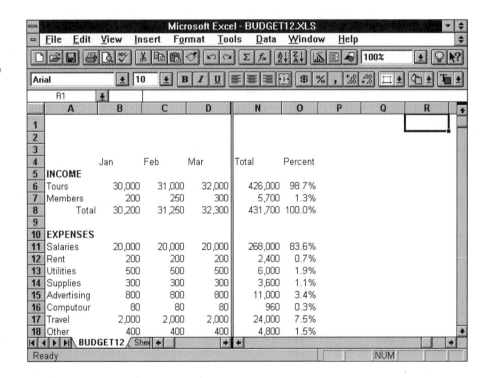

left of the split, and columns E through I at the right of the split. Splitting a worksheet creates two separate views of the worksheet. It is like having two monitors viewing the same worksheet. You can scroll each side independently of the other. Figure 5.5 shows the right side scrolled to display columns N and O. With this view you could make a change in the March numbers and see the effect on the totals. To split a worksheet vertically, you select the column to the right of where the split will occur and choose the **Split command** from

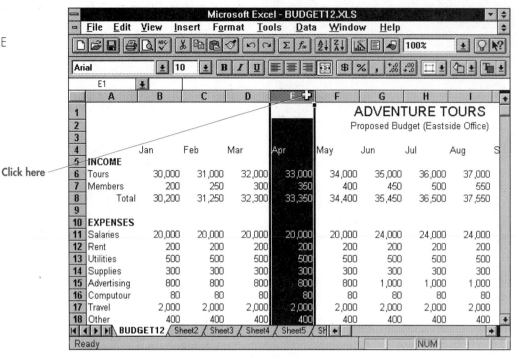

Click here

the Window menu. In this case you want the split to be to the right of column D, so you would choose column E. Complete the following steps to duplicate Figure 5.5:

1. **Click on E in the column headings to highlight column E (see Figure 5.6).**

2. **Click on Window in the menu bar.**

3. **Click on Split.**

The worksheet is split into two parts. You can move between the two parts by selecting cells in each one, and you can scroll each part separately from the other. Currently, the right side is selected. Use the ⟶ key to scroll this side of the split.

4. **Press ⟶ ten times to bring the total and percent columns into view.**

Notice that the right side scrolls while the left side remains unchanged. Now scroll the right side until the total column (N) is next to the March column (D).

5. **Press ⟶ three times.**

Your screen should resemble Figure 5.5. With this view you can make a change in the travel expense for March and see the effect on the total expenses. Change to full screen view to see the total expenses.

6. **Choose Full Screen from the View menu.**

Note the current total expenses, 320,760.

7. **Click on cell D17 (March travel expense).**

8. **Type 4500**

9. **Press ⟵Enter.**

The total expenses change to 323,260.

10. **On your own, change the advertising expense for February to 1200, and notice the change in the total expenses.**

The Window menu can be used to remove a split.

11. **Choose Remove Split from the Window menu.**

12. **Click on the Full Screen button to return to the normal view.**

13. **Close the workbook without saving the changes.**

The worksheet can be split horizontally by choosing a row number rather than a column letter. Further, if you select a cell before splitting a worksheet, the worksheet is split into four parts instead of two.

PRINTING LARGE WORKSHEETS

In addition to viewing large worksheets, you need to know how to print them. The amount of data you can print on a sheet of paper depends on the paper size, the margins, the font size, the column widths, and the worksheet orientation. (The orientation refers to the way the worksheet is printed on the page. It can be printed in the standard orientation, called **portrait**, or it can be printed sideways, called **landscape**. We will show examples of these later.) Figure 5.7 shows how the budget document is printed on two pages using the

5.7

The budget document printed on two pages

BUDGET12.XLS

ADVENTURE TOURS
Proposed Budget (Eastside Office)

	Jan	Feb	Mar	Apr	May	Jun	Jul	Aug
INCOME								
Tours	30,000	31,000	32,000	33,000	34,000	35,000	36,000	37,000
Members	200	250	300	350	400	450	500	550
Total	30,200	31,250	32,300	33,350	34,400	35,450	36,500	37,550
EXPENSES								
Salaries	20,000	20,000	20,000	20,000	20,000	24,000	24,000	24,000
Rent	200	200	200	200	200	200	200	200
Utilities	500	500	500	500	500	500	500	500
Supplies	300	300	300	300	300	300	300	300
Advertising	800	800	800	800	800	1,000	1,000	1,000
Computour	80	80	80	80	80	80	80	80
Travel	2,000	2,000	2,000	2,000	2,000	2,000	2,000	2,000
Other	400	400	400	400	400	400	400	400
Total	24,280	24,280	24,280	24,280	24,280	28,480	28,480	28,480
PROFIT	5,920	6,970	8,020	9,070	10,120	6,970	8,020	9,070

Page 1

BUDGET12.XLS

Sep	Oct	Nov	Dec	Total	Percent
38,000	39,000	40,000	41,000	426,000	98.7%
800	650	700	750	5,700	1.3%
38,800	39,650	40,700	41,750	431,700	100.0%
24,000	24,000	24,000	24,000	268,000	83.6%
200	200	200	200	2,400	0.7%
500	500	500	500	6,000	1.9%
300	300	300	300	3,600	1.1%
1,000	1,000	1,000	1,000	11,000	3.4%
80	80	80	80	960	0.3%
2,000	2,000	2,000	2,000	24,000	7.5%
400	400	400	400	4,800	1.5%
28,480	28,480	28,480	28,480	320,760	100.0%
10,120	11,170	12,220	13,270	110,940	

Page 2

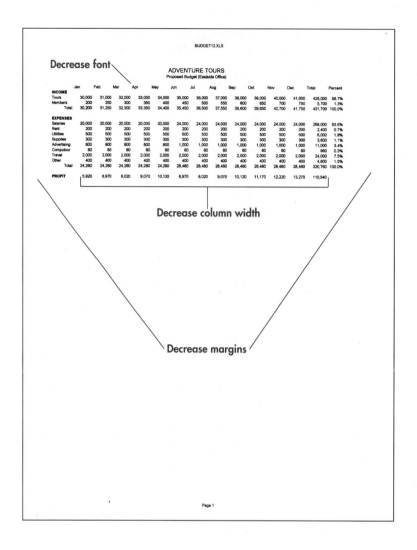

regular 8.5" by 11" paper and the default settings for the margins. Notice that columns A through I fit on the first page. Figure 5.8 shows the same worksheet printed on one page.

Although Excel allows you to change margins, font size, and column widths, the easiest way to reduce the number of pages it takes to print a large workbook is to change the Page options in the Page Setup dialog box. Figure 5.9 shows the dialog box. Some of the options are described below.

Orientation

- **Portrait**   Prints the workbook in the standard 8.5" wide by 11.5" long page layout.

- **Landscape**   Prints the workbook sideways (11.5" wide by 8.5" long).

Scaling

- **Adjust to:**   Allows you to enlarge or reduce the size of the workbook. This is similar to the Zoom command used earlier in the chapter. This feature may not work for all types of printers.

- **Fit to:** Automatically reduces the workbook to fit on the specified number of pages.

You will use the Fit to option to print the entire workbook on one page. Start by opening the workbook and displaying the print preview screen.

1. **Open budget12.xls and choose Print Preview from the File menu.**

Notice that the status line at the bottom of the screen says Page 1 of 2. You can click on the Next button to display the second page.

2. **Click on the Next button.**

3. **After viewing the second page, click on the Previous button.**

Now change the page setup to have the workbook printed on one page.

4. **Click on the Setup button.**

5. **If necessary, click on the Page tab to display the Page options.**

6. **Click on Fit to.**

Leave the number of pages set to 1. Your dialog box should resemble the one in Figure 5.9.

7. **Click on OK.**

The workbook now fits on one page. Notice that the status line says Page 1 of 1.

8. **Print the workbook.**

9. **Save the workbook as bgt_smal.**

10. **Close the workbook.**

PRINTING A WORKSHEET SIDEWAYS

The bgt_smal worksheet can print on one page, but the characters will be small, giving the printed document a cluttered appearance. Figure 5.10 shows the document printed sideways (landscape orientation) on the paper. This orientation allows you to print wide documents on one page. You can change the orientation using the Page Setup dialog box.

1. **Open budget12.**

2. **Choose Print Preview from the File menu.**

3. **Click on Setup.**

4. **If necessary, click on the Page tab.**

Notice the Orientation settings. Currently, the Portrait option is selected.

5. **Click on Landscape.**

6. **Click on OK.**

The print preview screen shows how the worksheet will print in landscape orientation. All but the percent column will fit on one page. Use the Fit to option in the Page Setup dialog box to have the workbook print on one page.

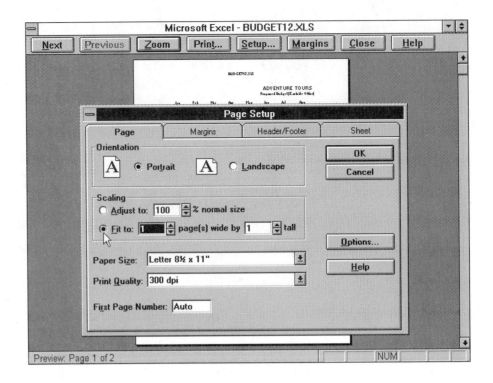

7. Click on the **S**etup button.

8. Click on Fit to in the Page section of the dialog box.

9. Click on OK.

Now the entire worksheet fits on the page.

CREATING HEADERS AND FOOTERS

Study Figure 5.10. Notice that the file name, BUDGET12.XLS, is displayed at the top of the page. This is a header. A **header** is text that prints at the top of each page of a document. Headers can be positioned at the left side, center, or right side of the page. You can enter any text that you want as a header. The default text and position for a header is the file name centered at the top of the page. Also notice the word *Page* followed by the page number positioned at the bottom center of the page. This is a footer. A **footer** is text that prints at the bottom of each page of a document. The default text for a footer is the word *Page* followed by the page number. You can make changes in headers and footers using the Page Setup dialog box. Figure 5.11 shows the changes you will make. The header is the date aligned at the left side of the page. The footer is the word *Page* followed by the page number aligned at the right side of the page. Complete the following steps to duplicate Figure 5.11:

1. From the print preview screen, click on **S**etup.

2. Click on the Header/Footer tab.

5.10

The document printed sideways (landscape orientation)

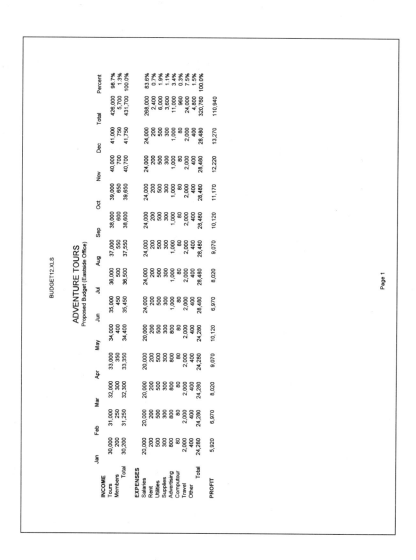

5.11

Changes to the header and footer

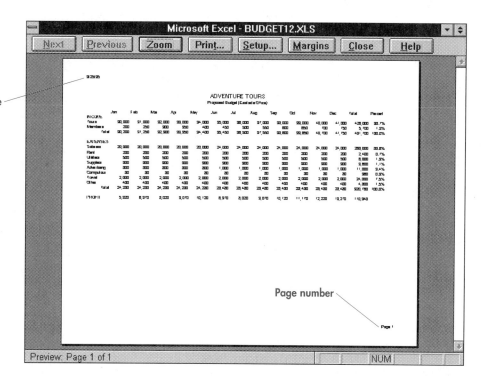

5.12

The default header and
footer displayed in the
Page Setup dialog box

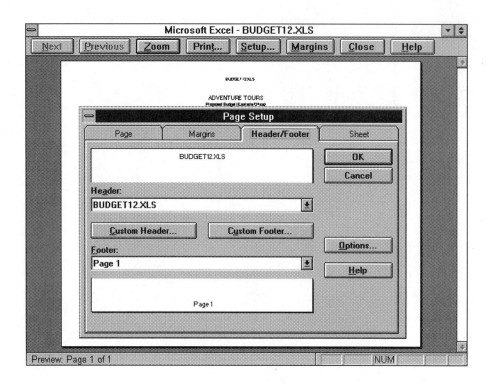

Figure 5.12 shows the Header/Footer section that displays the current header (BUDGET12.XLS) and footer (Page 1). Both the header and footer are centered across the page. You can create your own headers and footers by using the Custom Header and Custom Footer buttons.

3. **Click on the Custom Header button.**

The Header dialog box appears. There are three sections: left, center, and right. You select the section and then enter the text you want to appear in the header. Currently, &[File] appears in the Center Section box. The ampersand (&) is a symbol that indicates what follows is a code. File is the code for the file name. Thus, this entry specifies that the file name will be printed in the center of the page as a header. If the ampersand was not used, the word *File* would be printed rather than the file name. Notice the buttons in the middle of the dialog box. Several of these are shortcuts for entering codes, as indicated in Figure 5.13. Thus, if you wanted to have the file name appear at the right side of the page, you would select the Right Section box and click on the file name button. Then &[File] would appear in the Right Section box. Figure 5.13 shows the Header dialog box after deleting the entry in the Center Section box and entering the date code in the Left Section box. To delete an entry, you select it and press [Delete].

4. **Point to &[File].**

5. **Drag the mouse button to highlight the entry.**

6. **Press [Delete].**

7. **Point to inside the Left Section box.**

8. **Click the mouse button to display a cursor.**

9. **Click on the date button (see Figure 5.13).**

5.13

The Header dialog box
after changes have been
made to the header

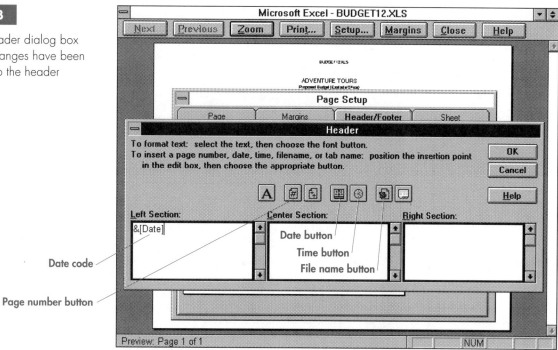

Now &[Date] is displayed in the Left Section box, indicating that the date will
be printed at the left of the page as a header.

10. Click on **OK** to exit the Header dialog box.

11. Click on **OK** in the Page Setup dialog box to return to the print
preview screen.

Notice that the date is displayed as a header. You can enlarge the display by
using the magnifying glass.

12. Point to the date with the magnifying glass.

13. Click the mouse button to enlarge the display.

14. Click the mouse button to return to the original view.

Now change the footer.

15. Display the Page Setup dialog box.

16. Click on the C**u**stom Footer button in the Header/Footer section.

The Footer dialog box shows the entry (Page &[Page]) that will display
the word *Page* followed by the page number. (&[Page] is the code for page
numbers.)

17. Delete the entry.

18. Click in the **R**ight Section box.

19. Type Page

20. Press the spacebar.

21. Click on the page number button (see Figure 5.13).

22. Return to the print preview screen.

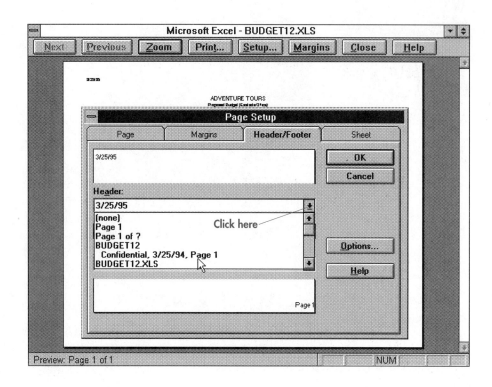

Your screen should resemble Figure 5.11.

23. **Print the document.**

In addition to creating your own custom headers and footers, you can select from several built-in ones.

24. **Choose Print Pre_view from the File menu.**

25. **Click on the _Setup button.**

26. **Click on the down arrow next to the He_ader list box (see Figure 5.14).**

27. **Use the up scroll arrow to view the built-in options.**

28. **Click on the option that says _Confidential_ followed by the current date and the page number.**

Notice how the sample changes.

29. **Click on the Cancel button to remove the changes.**

Before continuing, set the page orientation back to portrait.

30. **Choose the _Setup button.**

31. **Click on the Page tab.**

32. **Click on Por_trait.**

33. **Click on _Adjust to.**

34. **Change the scaling to 100%.**

35. **Click on OK.**

36. **Return to the worksheet.**

SPECIFYING A PAGE BREAK

Excel automatically inserts a **page break** based on the paper size and the margins. Figure 5.7 shows the two-page worksheet printed using the default page break. Notice that the first page would print out columns A through I (the months January through August). You can insert a page break to cause the worksheet to break at a different column. Figure 5.15 shows page one of the worksheet after inserting a page break at column H. Notice that the first page ends at column G (June). To insert a page break, you select the column (or row) that will start the next page and then choose the Page Break command from the Insert menu.

Before breaking this document, you need to change the alignment of the worksheet heading. The title, *Adventure Tours,* and subtitle, *Proposed Budget* (*Eastside Office*), are located in cells B1 and B2 and formatted to appear centered across the worksheet. Change the alignment of these titles.

1. **Select cells B1 and B2.**

2. **Click on the Align Left button on the Formatting toolbar.**

5.15

Page 1 of the worksheet after inserting a page break at column H

3/25/95

ADVENTURE TOURS
Proposed Budget (Eastside Office)

	Jan	Feb	Mar	Apr	May	Jun
INCOME						
Tours	30,000	31,000	32,000	33,000	34,000	35,000
Members	200	250	300	350	400	450
Total	30,200	31,250	32,300	33,350	34,400	35,450
EXPENSES						
Salaries	20,000	20,000	20,000	20,000	20,000	24,000
Rent	200	200	200	200	200	200
Utilities	500	500	500	500	500	500
Supplies	300	300	300	300	300	300
Advertising	800	800	800	800	800	1,000
Computour	80	80	80	80	80	80
Travel	2,000	2,000	2,000	2,000	2,000	2,000
Other	400	400	400	400	400	400
Total	24,280	24,280	24,280	24,280	24,280	28,480
PROFIT	5,920	6,970	8,020	9,070	10,120	6,970

Page 1

Now you can insert a page break without splitting the worksheet heading across two pages. Complete the following steps to insert the page break shown in Figure 5.15.

3. Select cell H1.

4. Click on Insert in the menu bar.

5. Click on Page Break.

Notice that a broken line appears between columns G and H. This line indicates a page break. Preview how the document will print.

6. Choose Print Preview from the File menu.

Now the first page ends at the June column.

7. Click on the Next button to view the second page.

8. Click on the Zoom button to enlarge the view.

SETTING PRINT TITLES

Notice on page two of the worksheet that there are no titles to indicate what the numbers represent. For example, are the 300 values supplies, utilities, or advertising? You can cause the titles in column A to reappear on the second (or any subsequent) page by using the Page Setup dialog box from the File menu. You must use the Page Setup command from the File menu to establish **print titles**.

1. Click on the Zoom button to reduce the view.

2. Return to the worksheet.

3. Choose Page Setup from the File menu.

4. Click on the Sheet tab.

The Print Titles option allows you to specify the location where the titles are to appear on each page. You can specify titles located in rows, columns, or both. In this case you will need to specify A1:A21 as the cells containing the titles for the rows. Figure 5.16 shows the complete entry.

5. Point to the Columns to Repeat at Left box.

6. Click the mouse button to display a cursor.

7. Type A1:A21

Your dialog box should resemble Figure 5.16.

8. Click on OK.

Now view how the document will print.

9. Choose Print Preview from the File menu.

10. Click on Next to display the second page.

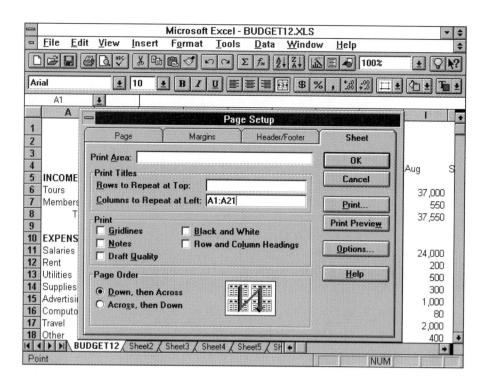

Notice that the row titles are displayed and will print on the second page.

11. **Return to the worksheet.**

Now remove the page break.

12. **Click on cell H1.**

13. **Click on Insert in the menu bar.**

14. **Click on Remove Page Break.**

PRINTING A PART OF THE WORKSHEET

In this section you will learn how to select a part of the worksheet to print. Figure 5.17 shows a printout of only the income numbers for the first seven months. You can print any part of the worksheet by highlighting the desired cells and choosing the Selection option from the Print dialog box. You first need to select the desired area.

1. **Select cells A4 through H8.**

2. **Choose Print from the File menu.**

3. **Click on Selection in the Print What area of the dialog box.**

4. **Click on the Print Preview button to see how the selected area would print.**

5. **When done viewing, return to the worksheet.**

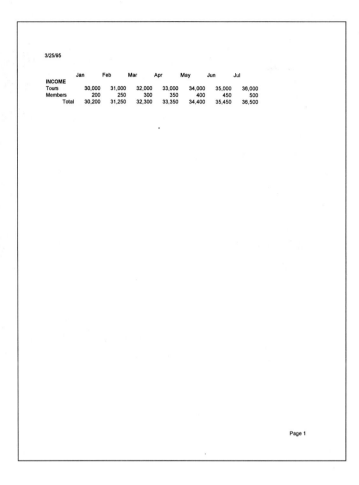

	Jan	Feb	Mar	Apr	May	Jun	Jul
3/25/95

INCOME							
Tours	30,000	31,000	32,000	33,000	34,000	35,000	36,000
Members	200	250	300	350	400	450	500
Total	30,200	31,250	32,300	33,350	34,400	35,450	36,500

Page 1

PRINTING NONADJACENT COLUMNS AND ROWS

Excel allows you to **hide cells** from view. This can be useful if you want to print selected rows or columns that are not adjacent. Figure 5.18 shows the worksheet after hiding columns B through M. The process is to select the desired columns and choose the Hide option from the Format menu.

1. Point to the column heading B.

2. Hold down the mouse button and drag the pointer to select columns B through M.

3. Choose Column from the Format menu.

4. Click on Hide.

The worksheet appears with the selected columns hidden. You can also print the document this way.

5. Choose Print Preview from the File menu.

6. After viewing the document, return to the worksheet.

7. Close the workbook without saving it.

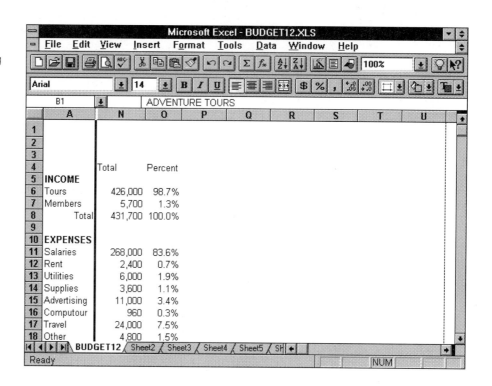

KEY TERMS

Fit Selection option   hide cells   print titles
footer   landscape   Split command
Full Screen command   page break   Zoom command
header   portrait

REVIEW QUESTIONS

1. The _____ command can be used to change the magnification of the worksheet.

2. The _____ option uses the whole screen to display the worksheet data.

3. **T F**   The Split command allows you to view two different parts of the worksheet at one time.

4. The two page orientations are _____ and _____.

5. A _____ is text that will print at the top of each page of a document.

6. The Page Break command is found in the _____ menu.

7. **T F** The Print Titles option allows you to print row or column headings on each page of a document.

8. **T F** Cells that are hidden will not be displayed onscreen but they will print.

PROJECTS

On the data disk is a file called gw_trek.xls. This workbook contains the names and addresses of members who will be going on a trek of the Great Wall of China. The workbook also contains the amounts each person has paid to date and what money, if any, is owed to Adventure Tours. You will use this workbook to complete the projects.

1. Open gw_trek.xls and complete the following:
   a. Using the Zoom command:
      ■ Which is the highest standard magnification option that can be used to view the entire document?
      ■ Which column headings are displayed when you choose the 200% magnification?
   b. With 100% magnification and using the print preview screen:
      ■ What columns are displayed on the first page?
      ■ What columns are displayed on the second page?
   c. Change the header to your name and the current date, and display it on the left side of the page. Change the footer (Page &[Page]) to the left side of the page. Preview and print the document using landscape orientation, and then save the document as ch5_p1.

2. Open gw_trek.xls. Set a page break so that only the name and address columns are printed on the first page. Change the header to your name and the date in the middle of the page. Change the footer to the word *page* and the page number on the right side of the page. Set print titles so that the last names and first names print on the second page. Preview the document, and then save the document as ch5_p2.

3. Open gw_trek.xls. Change the header to your name and the date in the middle of the page. Change the footer to the word *page* and the page number on the right side of the page. Preview the document, and print it with only the document title, column headings, and the names and addresses of members in Seattle displayed. Save the document as ch5_p3.

4. Open gw_trek.xls. Hide all the columns except for those containing the names, addresses, and amount due. Change the header to your name and the date in the middle of the page. Change the footer to the word *page* and the page number on the right side of the page. Preview and print the document, and then save the document as ch5_p4.

6

Working with Multiple Documents and Other Applications

- Display several worksheet documents at one time

- Copy data from one worksheet document to another

- Link worksheet documents

- Copy an Excel document to a word processing document

Adventure Tours has two offices, Downtown and Eastside. Throughout the year the company develops various worksheets such as budgets and income statements for each office. At the end of the year, they need to combine some of the worksheets to determine how the overall company is doing. Figure 6.1 shows three worksheets, downtown, eastside, and company. The company document was developed by copying the headings and then linking the numeric data from the other two documents.

6.1

Two worksheets combined to create a linked third worksheet

DOWNTOWN			
	A	B	C
1	**Adventure Tours**		
2	Downtown Office		
3			
4	INCOME		
5	Tours	450000	
6	Members	5617	
7	Total	455617	
8			
9	EXPENSES		
10	Salaries	360283	
11	Rent	8000	
12	Utilities	4293	
13	Ads	12093	
14	Travel	33566	
15	Other	5382	
16	Total	423617	
17			
18	PROFIT	32000	

+

EASTSIDE			
	A	B	C
1	**Adventure Tours**		
2	Eastside Office		
3			
4	INCOME		
5	Tours	330000	
6	Members	4314	
7	Total	334314	
8			
9	EXPENSES		
10	Salaries	269934	
11	Rent	6000	
12	Utilities	3390	
13	Ads	8293	
14	Travel	21843	
15	Other	3854	
16	Total	313314	
17			
18	PROFIT	21000	

=

COMPANY			
	A	B	C
1	**Adventure Tours**		
2	Company		
3			
4	INCOME		
5	Tours	780000	
6	Members	9931	
7	Total	789931	
8			
9	EXPENSES		
10	Salaries	630217	
11	Rent	14000	
12	Utilities	7683	
13	Ads	20386	
14	Travel	55409	
15	Other	9236	
16	Total	736931	
17			
18	PROFIT	53000	

USING WORKBOOKS

Until now you have been working with one **worksheet** at a time. Excel 5.0 allows you to work with multiple worksheets in a single workbook. A **workbook** is like an electronic three-ring binder that helps you organize your work. Figure 6.2 shows the first worksheet (downtown) of a workbook (co_proft.xls) that contains two sheets. Each worksheet has a **sheet tab** with the worksheet name (downtown, eastside). You will combine these two worksheets into an overall company worksheet as shown in Figure 6.1. This involves three steps. First you will insert a new worksheet into the workbook. Second you copy the headings in the downtown worksheet to the new worksheet. Third you add the numbers in the downtown and eastside sheets to create the numbers in the new worksheet. Start by opening the co_proft.xls workbook.

1. **Start Excel 5.0.**

2. **Open co_proft.xls.**

The workbook appears with the downtown worksheet displayed. Now take a moment to use the worksheet tabs to view the eastside worksheet.

3. **Click on the EASTSIDE sheet tab.**

6.2

The co_proft.xls workbook with two worksheets, downtown and eastside

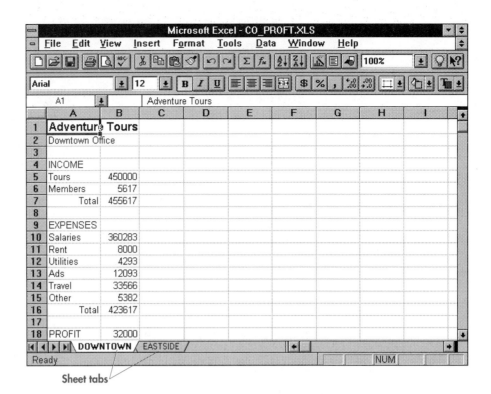

Sheet tabs

Notice that the layout for the two sheets is the same. Only the numbers and the office names differ. Return to the downtown worksheet and insert a new worksheet for the company totals.

4. Click on the DOWNTOWN sheet tab.

5. Click on Insert in the menu bar.

6. Click on Worksheet.

A new blank worksheet appears. Notice the new sheet tab, Sheet1. Now copy the headings in the downtown worksheet to Sheet1.

COPYING DATA FROM ONE WORKSHEET TO ANOTHER

To copy data from one worksheet to another, you display the worksheet with the data to be copied, and then highlight the data and use the Copy and Paste commands from the Edit menu. Start by displaying the downtown worksheet.

1. Click on the DOWNTOWN sheet tab to display the downtown worksheet.

2. Select cells A1 through A18 in the downtown worksheet.

3. Click on Edit in the menu bar.

4. Click on Copy.

5. Click on the Sheet1 tab.

6. Choose Paste from the Edit menu.

The headings are copied to the blank worksheet. Now change the subheading, *Eastside Office*, to *Company*.

7. **Select A2 in the Sheet1 worksheet.**

8. **Type** Company

9. **Press** ⏎Enter.

Next you will combine the numbers in the downtown and eastside worksheets to obtain the numbers for the company worksheet. This is done by linking the worksheets.

LINKING WORKSHEETS

Excel allows you to **link** cells from various worksheets. Figure 6.3 shows how the tours incomes from the downtown and eastside offices are linked to the company worksheet. In effect, you are adding the two office incomes to obtain the company income. A formula is used to create the link. The format for the formula is:

=filename!cellrange

- ▪ = indicates a formula.

- ▪ filename is the name of the worksheet containing the cells to be linked.

- ▪ ! separates the file name from the cell range.

- ▪ cellrange is the cell(s) that is to be linked.

6.3

The tours income from the eastside and downtown worksheets linked to the company worksheet

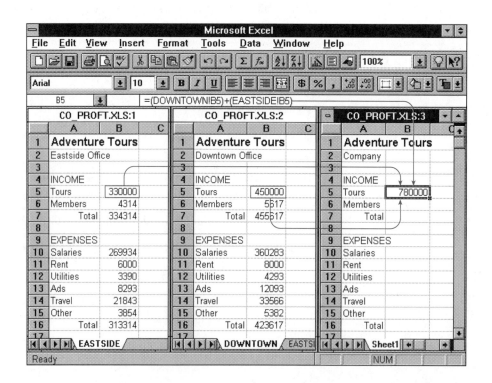

EXCEL 5.0 FOR WINDOWS

The formula for the current example is:

$$=(downtown!B5)+(eastside!B5)$$

This formula says take the number in cell B5 of the downtown worksheet and add it to the number in cell B5 of the eastside worksheet. (*Note:* The parentheses are used to separate the two major parts of the formula and to help with readability.) Now enter this formula into cell B5 of the company worksheet.

1. Select cell B5 of the company (Sheet1) worksheet.
2. Type =(downtown!B5)+(eastside!B5)
3. Click on the enter box on the formula bar.

The number 780000 is displayed in cell B5. This formula can be copied for the members income category.

4. Copy the entry in cell B5 to cell B6.
5. Select cell B7.
6. Use the AutoSum button to add cells B5 and B6.
7. Select cell B10.
8. On your own, enter the formula to link the salaries.
9. Copy the formula to the other expenses.
10. Select cell B16.
11. Total the expenses.
12. Select cell B18.
13. Subtract the expenses total from the income total to determine the profit.

Now rename Sheet1 to company.

14. Click on Format in the menu bar.
15. Click on Sheet.
16. Click on Rename.
17. Type COMPANY
18. Click on OK.

Your worksheet should resemble Figure 6.4. Now save and print the company worksheet.

19. Make sure the company worksheet is selected.
20. Choose Save As from the File menu.
21. Save the workbook as co_prft2.xls to the appropriate disk drive.
22. Print the document.

To illustrate how these worksheets are linked, change the income for the eastside office to 400000, and see the effect on the company worksheet. The company profit before this change is 53000.

23. Change the tours income to 400000 for the eastside office.

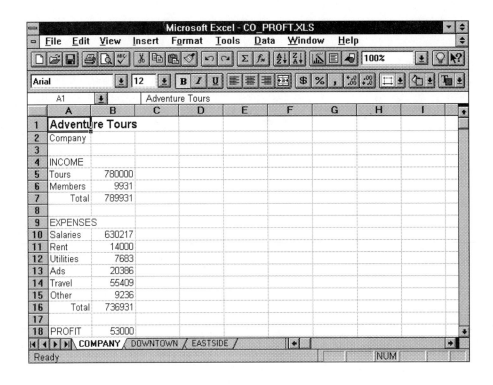

24. Display the company worksheet.

The company profit changes to 123000.

COPYING WORKSHEET DATA TO A WORD PROCESSING DOCUMENT

In this section you will learn how to combine documents created in different applications. Figure 6.5 shows a word processing document, a memo, that includes an Excel worksheet. The memo was developed using the **Write** application that comes with the Windows program. You will duplicate Figure 6.5. Start by opening the Write application. This can be done by using the **Switch To option** from the control-menu box.

1. Click on the control-menu box (see Figure 6.6).

2. Click on S_witch To.

A list of open windows appears. You need to switch to the Program Manager.

3. Double-click on Program Manager.

4. Double-click on the Accessories program group icon.

5. Double-click on the Write icon.

6. If necessary, maximize the Write window.

Now open the file called memo.wri.

7. Choose O_pen from the File menu.

A word processing
document that includes
an Excel worksheet

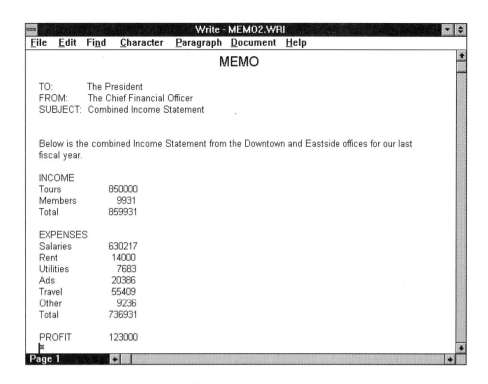

The control-menu box

Control-menu box —

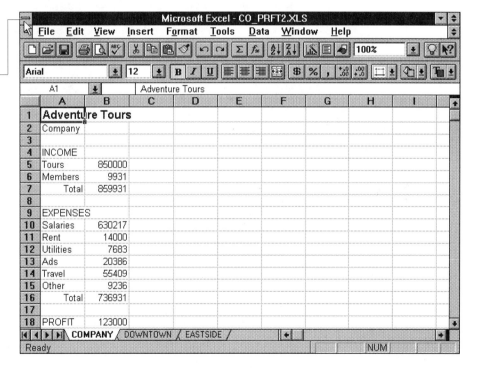

8. **Type** a:memo **(or** b:memo**).**

9. **Press** ⎯Enter .

After the memo appears:

10. **Press** Ctrl + End **to move the cursor to the end of the document.**

Now you can switch to the worksheet and copy the data to the memo.

11. Click on the control-menu box.

12. Click on Switch To.

13. Double-click on Microsoft Excel - CO_PRFT2.XLS.

14. Select cells A4 through B18 on the company worksheet.

15. Choose Copy from the Edit menu.

16. On your own, switch to the memo.

17. Choose Paste from the Edit menu.

18. Press Page Up.

The selected worksheet data is copied to the memo. Notice that some of the numbers are not aligned. This is because the data from the worksheet is aligned at tab positions in the Write document. You can use the Tab key and the spacebar to align the numbers. This is done by positioning the cursor immediately in front of a number and pressing Tab or the spacebar.

19. Align the numbers on your own.

20. Save the document as memo2.

21. Use the Print command from the File menu to print the document.

22. Use the File menu to exit the Write program.

23. Close the company worksheet without saving the changes.

This completes the section on copying worksheet data to a word processing program.

CHAPTER REVIEW

KEY TERMS

| link | sheet tab | worksheet |
| Switch To option | workbook | Write |

REVIEW QUESTIONS

1. To display the worksheet name on the worksheet tab, choose the _____ command from the _____ menu and then select the _____ option.

2. **T F**   An Excel workbook can contain more than one worksheet.

3. Assume you have two worksheets, budget and co_budget. What is the formula to link cell D15 from these two worksheets to a third worksheet? _____.

4. The _____ and _____ commands from the Edit menu are used to copy data from an Excel workbook to a Write application document.

5. The Switch To option is found in the _____ box.

PROJECTS

1. On the data disk is a file called co_forct. This workbook contains two worksheets that compare the actual and forecasted income, expenses, and profit for the eastside and downtown offices. The worksheets are named dntn_for and east_for. Open the co_forct workbook, and create a company worksheet that combines the data. Copy the headings and link the numeric data. Format the percentages to display the percent sign. Save the workbook as ch6_p1, and then print the company worksheet. Test the link by changing a number in the east_for worksheet and noticing the results in the company worksheet.

2. On the data disk is a workbook called survey.xls. This workbook has three worksheets, called survy_w1, survy_w2, and survy_w3, which contain the results of a three-week survey by Adventure Tours. Open this workbook and combine the data into a new worksheet. Copy the headings and link the numeric data. Insert an appropriate title on the worksheet and add a name to the worksheet tab. Save the workbook as ch6_p2, and then print the new worksheet. Test the link by changing a number in the survy_w1 worksheet and noticing the results in the new worksheet.

3. Using Write (or another Windows word processing application), develop a memo from you to the company employees. In the memo refer to the survey results (shown in workbook ch6_p2). Then copy the new worksheet you created in Project 2 to the memo. Save the memo as ch6_p3, and then print the memo.

Appendix
Excel 5.0 for Windows
Quick Reference

This appendix contains a quick reference to Microsoft Excel 5.0 for Windows. It describes the procedures most frequently used in Microsoft Excel 5.0 for Windows. The appendix also includes the steps used to turn the Transition Navigation Keys on and off and a description of the Standard and Formatting toolbars.

PROCEDURES

Centering a heading across the workbook

- select the heading and the cells it will be centered across
- click on the Center Across Columns button on the Formatting toolbar

Centering data within a cell

- select the cell
- click on the Center alignment button on the Formatting toolbar

Charts

Changing the appearance

- double-click on the chart to select it
- click on the desired chart object (e.g., the title) to select it
- use the menu commands to make the desired changes

Changing the type

- double-click on the chart to select it
- choose AutoFormat from the Format menu
- choose the desired chart type from the dialog box

Creating

- select the cells that contain the data to be used in the chart
- click on the ChartWizard tool on the Standard toolbar

- drag the pointer to draw a box in a blank area of the workbook
- complete the five ChartWizard dialog boxes

Deleting

- click on the chart to select it
- press Delete

Opening

- use the Open command from the File menu to open the workbook used in creating the chart

Printing with the worksheet data

- choose Print from the File menu

Printing without the worksheet data

- double-click on the chart to select it
- choose Print from the File menu

Saving the chart and the workbook

- choose the Save As command from the File menu
- specify the disk drive and file name

Closing a workbook

- choose Close from the File menu

Column widths, changing

- click on the column letter
- choose Column from the Format menu
- choose the Width command
- specify the desired column width

  or

- point to the line between the column letters
- when the pointer changes to a double-arrow, hold down the mouse button and drag the column line to the desired position

Copying text and numbers

- Select the data
- hold down Ctrl
- place the mouse pointer on the border of the selected cells
- hold down the mouse button and drag the data to the desired location
- release the mouse button

  or

- choose Copy from the Edit menu (or click on the Copy button on the Standard toolbar)

- select the new location
- choose Paste from the Edit menu (or click on the Paste button on the Standard toolbar)

Copying formulas

(*Note:* Cell addresses will automatically be changed as the formula is copied to a new location. If a part of the formula needs to remain the same, you must specify an absolute cell address by using $ signs in the cell address, e.g., $A$5.)

- use the process specified for copying text and numbers

Deleting data in a worksheet

- select the cell(s)
- press `Delete`

Formatting numbers

- select the cell(s)
- choose Cells from the Format menu
- click on the Number tab
- specify the desired format

Inserting a column

- select a cell in the desired column
- choose Columns from the Insert menu

Inserting a row

- select a cell in the desired row
- choose Rows from the Insert menu

Moving text and numbers

- select the data
- place the mouse pointer on the border of the selected cells
- hold down the mouse button and drag the data to the new location
- release the mouse button

    or

- choose Cut from the Edit menu (or click on the Cut button on the Standard toolbar)
- select the new location
- choose Paste from the Edit menu (or click on the Paste button on the Standard toolbar)

Opening a new (blank) workbook

- choose New from the File menu

Opening a previously saved workbook

- choose Open from the File menu
- in the dialog box specify the disk drive and the file name

Previewing a worksheet before printing

- choose Print Preview from the File menu (or click on the Print Preview button on the Standard toolbar)

Printing a worksheet

(*Note:* It is advisable to preview the worksheet before printing it by choosing Print Preview from the File menu.)

- choose Print from the File menu (or click on the Print button on the Standard toolbar)

Printing a worksheet sideways

- choose Page Setup from the File menu
- click on the Page tab
- click on Landscape

Saving a workbook

- choose Save As from the File menu
- in the dialog box specify the disk drive and the file name

Selecting a cell

- point to the cell
- click the mouse button

Selecting a group (range) of cells

- point to the first cell in the range (upper-left corner)
- hold down the mouse button and drag the pointer to the end of the range
- release the mouse button

Starting Microsoft Excel 5.0 for Windows

- start Windows
- double-click on the program group icon that contains the Microsoft Excel 5.0 for Windows application icon
- double-click on the Microsoft Excel 5.0 for Windows application icon

Quitting Microsoft Excel 5.0 for Windows

- choose Exit from the File menu or double-click on the control-menu box

TRANSITION NAVIGATION KEYS

There are two settings that will affect the movement of the cell selector, Move Selection after Enter and Transition Navigation Keys. Both of these are found in the Options dialog box in the Tools menu.

When turned on, the Move Selection after Enter setting will cause the cell selector to move down one row. For example, if you make an entry in cell B5 and then press ⌐Enter⌐, the cell selector will move to B6. To turn this setting on and off, you choose Options from the Tools menu. Then click on the Edit tab and click on Move Selection after Enter. An X will appear when the setting is turned on.

The Transition Navigation Keys setting will change many of the other cell selector keys. When this setting is turned off, ⌐Home⌐ will move the cell selector to the first column in the current row. When this setting is turned on, ⌐Home⌐ will move the cell selector to cell A1. To turn this setting on and off, you choose Options from the Tools menu. Then click on the Transition tab and click on Transition Navigation Keys. An X will appear when the setting is turned on.

THE STANDARD AND FORMATTING TOOLBARS

Excel provides several toolbars including the Standard, Formatting, Drawing, and Chart toolbars. Toolbars can be displayed or hidden using the Toolbar command from the View menu. The following labels the tools on the Standard and Formatting toolbars.

QR-1

The Standard and Formatting toolbars

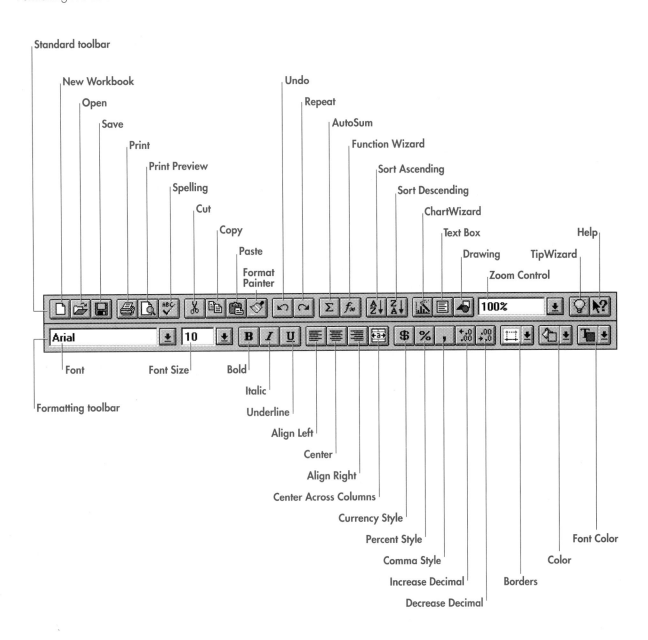

Glossary

Absolute cell reference   A cell reference that will not change when it is used in a formula that is copied to another location.

Active cell   The selected cell. The first cell selected in a block of cells.

AutoSum button   A button on the Standard toolbar that is used to automatically add values in cells.

Book1   The name given to an Excel workbook document that has not been saved.

Cell   The area where a row and column intersect.

Chart   A drawing showing the relationships among numbers.

ChartWizard   An Excel tool that leads you through the process of developing a chart.

Clipboard   A holding area in Windows containing data that has been cut or copied.

Column headings   The letters that identify columns.

Commands   Options such as Print, Save, and Copy that are used when working with Excel.

Control-menu box   The box in the upper-left corner of a window that is used primarily to close a window or switch to another application.

Data series   The series of numbers used to create a chart.

Document   The name given to an Excel worksheet.

Drag-and-drop   A method for moving or copying data in a worksheet or between worksheets.

File   An Excel workbook document that has been saved.

File name   The name given to an Excel document when it is saved.

Font   A type design such as New Times Roman or Arial.

Footers   Information that is printed at the bottom of each page of an Excel worksheet.

Formula bar   The area of the window that displays the cell entry.

Functions   Preset Excel formulas that perform arithmetic, statistical, and financial operations on the values in a worksheet.

Headers   Information that is printed at the top of each page of an Excel worksheet.

Landscape   The orientation of a worksheet document that will cause it to print horizontally (sideways).

Linking   A process of setting up relationships among the cells of different worksheets.

Maximize button   The button used to enlarge a window to the size of the screen.

Menu bar   The area of a window that displays the menu names.

Microsoft Excel 5.0   A Windows spreadsheet application program.

Microsoft Windows A program that provides a graphical environment for working with the computer.

Minimize button The button used to reduce a window to an icon.

Pointer The onscreen symbol that moves as the mouse is moved.

Portrait The orientation of a workbook document that will cause it to print vertically.

Reference bar The area of the window that displays the name of the selected cell.

Restore button The button used to restore a window to its previous size.

Row headings The numbers that identify rows.

Scroll bars The vertical and horizontal bars used to scroll the window to view different parts of the worksheet.

Spreadsheet A computer program used to develop reports and charts that include numbers and calculations.

SUM function A function used to add the values in cells.

Title bar The highlighted bar at the top of a window that identifies the program and/or the workbook document displayed in the window.

Toolbars A series of buttons that provide shortcuts to commands.

Workbook The part of the Excel program that contains the worksheets. A workbook is like an electronic three-ring binder that holds one or more worksheets.

Worksheet The part of a workbook that contains the data (numbers, text, formulas).

Write A word processing application that comes with the Windows program.

X axis The horizontal line of a column or line chart that usually displays a timeline or labels.

.xls A file name extension automatically appended to an Excel document when it is saved.

Y axis The vertical line of a column or line chart that usually displays units of measurement.

Index